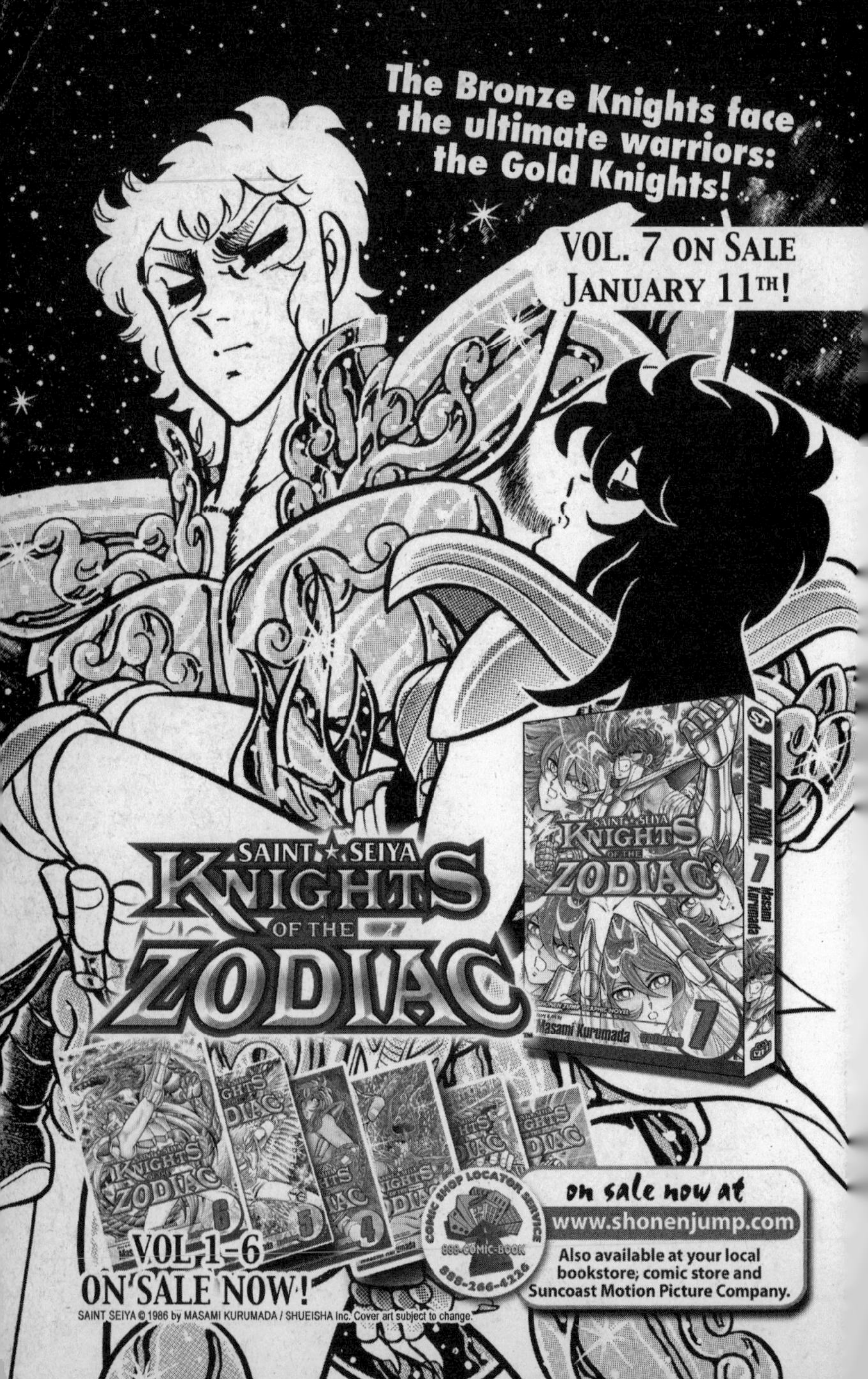
The Bronze Knights face the ultimate warriors: the Gold Knights!
VOL. 7 ON SALE JANUARY 11TH!
SAINT SEIYA KNIGHTS OF THE ZODIAC
VOL 1-6 ON SALE NOW!
on sale now at
www.shonenjump.com
Also available at your local bookstore, comic store and Suncoast Motion Picture Company.
COMIC SHOP LOCATOR SERVICE
888-COMIC-BOOK
888-266-4226
SAINT SEIYA © 1986 by MASAMI KURUMADA / SHUEISHA Inc. Cover art subject to change.

I'M NEVER GOING TO MAKE ALL OF YOU HAPPY, AM I.
YOU ASK TOO MUCH. KNOW YOUR LIMITS.

和月伸宏

NOBUHIRO WATSUKI

ABOUT THE "SECRET LIFE OF CHARACTERS"

IN WRITING ABOUT SAITŌ HAJIME ("SECRET LIVES [27]," VOLUME 7), ONCE AGAIN I RECEIVED READER RESPONSE. TO WIT: "ARE YOU TRYING TO PICK FIGHTS WITH YOUR READERS OR WHAT? IS IT REALLY IN YOUR BEST INTEREST TO DO SO?" ...UM, OKAY. LOOK. THE "SECRET LIVES" FEATURE ITSELF IS PROBABLY NOT IN A MANGA ARTIST'S BEST INTEREST. YOU'RE GETTING THE INSIDE SCOOP ON STUFF THAT WOULD ORDINARILY NEVER BE REVEALED. IT'S IMPOSSIBLE TO MAKE *EVERYONE* HAPPY. IT'S A DIFFICULT THING, FAN SERVICE.

Rurouni Kenshin, which has found fans not only in Japan but around the world, first made its appearance in 1992, as an original short story in ***Weekly Shonen Jump Special***. Later rewritten and published as a regular, continuing ***Jump*** series in 1994, ***Rurouni Kenshin*** ended serialization in 1999 but continued in popularity, as evidenced by the 2000 publication of ***Yahiko no Sakabatô*** ("Yahiko's Reversed-Edge Sword") in ***Weekly Shonen Jump***. His most current work, ***Busô Renkin*** ("Armored Alchemist"), began publication in June 2003, also in ***Jump***.

RUROUNI KENSHIN
VOL. 9: ARRIVAL IN KYOTO
The SHONEN JUMP Graphic Novel Edition

STORY AND ART BY
NOBUHIRO WATSUKI

English Adaptation/Gerard Jones
Translation/Kenichiro Yagi
Touch-up Art & Lettering/Steve Dutro
Cover, Graphics & Layout/Sean Lee
Editor/Avery Gotoh

Supervising Editor/Kit Fox
Managing Editor/Elizabeth Kawasaki
Director of Production/Noboru Watanabe
Editorial Director/Alvin Lu
Executive Vice President & Editor in Chief/Hyoe Narita
Sr. Director of Licensing & Acquisitions/Rika Inouye
Vice President of Sales & Marketing/Liza Coppola
Vice President of Strategic Development/Yumi Hoashi
Publisher/Seiji Horibuchi

Printed in the U.S.A.

Published by VIZ, LLC
P.O. Box 77010
San Francisco, CA 94107

SHONEN JUMP Graphic Novel Edition
10 9 8 7 6 5 4 3 2 1
First printing, November 2004

www.viz.com

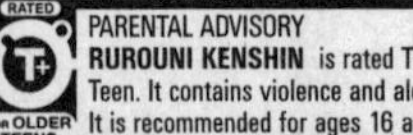

SHONEN JUMP GRAPHIC NOVEL

CAST
緋村剣心（人斬り抜刀斎）
Himura Kenshin
(Hitokiri Battōsai)
神谷 薫
Kamiya Kaoru
明神弥彦
Myōjin Yahiko
相楽左之助
Sagara Sanosuke
斎藤 一
Saitō Hajime
巻町 操
Makimachi Misao
志々雄真実
Shishio Makoto

Once he was *hitokiri*, an assassin, called Battōsai. His name was legend among the pro-Imperialist or "patriot" warriors who launched the Meiji Era. Now, Himura Kenshin is *rurouni*, a wanderer, and carries a reversed-edge sakabatō to prohibit himself from killing.

THUS FAR

Ōkubo Toshimichi, head of the government's "Internal Affairs," tries to hire Kenshin to assassinate Shishio Makoto, the successor to "Hitokiri Battōsai." But it is Ōkubo who is assassinated, and Kenshin sets out for Kyoto to find his killers... despite the protests of Kaoru and the others. Kenshin says his farewells to Kaoru alone, declining the company of Saitō Hajime—an intelligence agent for the police and an ex-Shinsengumi—and sets out, on foot, on the East Sea Road. Through a strange twist of fate, he meets Makimachi Misao, a girl who admires a man Kenshin fought once before—Shinomori Aoshi, "Okashira" or "Head" of the Kyoto-based Oniwabanshū spy clan. While taking a shortcut through the forest, the two find an injured man and unconscious boy. The man begs Kenshin to save his village, then dies. Kenshin hears from the boy that his village is occupied by Shishio's men. Kenshin goes to the village to save the boy's parents, only to find their bodies strung up before him. The boy howls in sorrow. Suddenly, Shishio's men show up in order to rid the village of "intruders." Misao and the boy are saved—by Saitō Hajime.

CONTENTS

RUROUNI KENSHIN
Meiji Swordsman Romantic Story
BOOK NINE: ARRIVAL IN KYOTO

WOK
THOG
HO!
THIS POLICE-MAN...
...KNOWS KENSHIN ...?
Act 67
Birth of a Small Champion
OH-H-H YEAH... HIMURA!
WSH
OHHH!!
YAH

Act 67
Birth of a Small Champion

UHH...
DOM
WOW
HE'S NOT EVEN OUT OF BREATH...
HEY.
WHAT ARE YOU WASTING TIME HERE FOR?
TP
!
SAITŌ...

WHY HAVE YOU COME?
DOING MY JOB.

A REPORT FROM ONE OF MY MEN SAID THAT SHISHIO IS HERE.
WE HAVE A LITTLE TIME BEFORE FORCES GATHER IN KYOTO, SO I CAME TO LOOK.
BUT HE'S NOWHERE TO BE FOUND.

COULD ...
...THAT BOY'S BROTHER BE THE POLICE AGENT...?
BOY?

TP
...RIGHT. MISHIMA EI'ICHIRŌ IS ORIGINALLY FROM SHINGETSU VILLAGE.
I SENT HIM, THINKING HE WOULDN'T RAISE TOO MUCH SUSPICION.
BUT HE MUST HAVE BEEN FOUND OUT. HE TRIED TO AT LEAST SAVE HIS FAMILY, BUT...

READ THIS WAY

A FOOLISH BOY.
HE SHOULD HAVE WAITED FOR MY ARRIVAL.

SNORT
HEY YOU. IS THAT ANY WAY TO TALK ABOUT THE DEAD?!
ROWR!
...MM? AND WHO IS THIS...

...WEASEL GIRL?
!

READ THIS WAY

EEE! I'LL KILL YOU!!
GRRRR
TAKE THIS, YOU-!
IT'S HIS WAY. LET HIM MAKE YOU MAD, AND IT'LL NEVER END.
HMPH.
BESIDES ...

...WE'VE GOT TO TAKE THEM DOWN.

...AND BURY THEM.

...TRUE.

STOP!

YOU CAN'T TAKE THEM DOWN!
GLARE
!

IF WE TOUCH THOSE BODIES AND ANGER SENKAKU...
...THE PEOPLE OF THIS VILLAGE WILL SUFFER!

UNTIL SENKAKU PERMITS IT...
JAB
...LEAVE THEM ALONE.

READ THIS WAY

WHAT ARE YOU SAYING?!
THEY ARE THE "PEOPLE OF THE VILLAGE"!!
ARE YOU SAYING YOU'LL OBEY THIS SENKAKU EVEN WHEN HE TREATS YOU LIKE THIS?!
IF WE OPPOSE SENKAKU, WE'RE GIVEN DEATH...
...WHILE, IF WE SUBMIT TO HIM, WE HAVE LIFE, AT LEAST.
IT'S BEST FOR THE VILLAGE NOT TO TAKE MATTERS ANY FURTHER. YOU STRANGERS...
...AND THE MISHIMA FAMILY... MUST LEAVE THE VILLAGE NOW.
EIJI.
DO YOU HEAR?
YOU...

GRAB!

DON'T GET ANGRY.

FEW ARE WILLING TO RISK THEIR LIVES TO PROTECT THE PRIDE AND RESPECT OF OTHER PEOPLE.

MOST ARE CONTENT TO LIVE. LIKE LIVESTOCK.

THEY NEED NEITHER PRIDE, NOR RESPECT.

SAY WHAT YOU WANT.
MUTTER
WHAT DOES A STRANGER KNOW?
MUTTER
MUTTER

IT'S ALL BECAUSE THE POLICE ARE WEAK, ANYWAY.
MUTTER
MUTTER
THAT'S RIGHT!

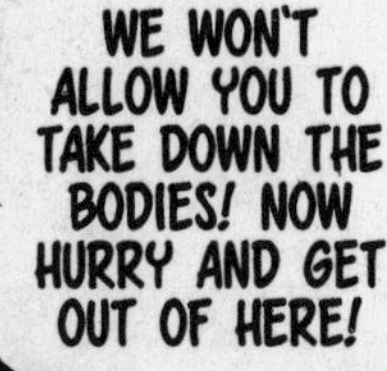

WE WON'T ALLOW YOU TO TAKE DOWN THE BODIES! NOW HURRY AND GET OUT OF HERE!

Tp

HIMURA!

!!
WH-WHAT ARE YOU DOING...?!
SHP
AWRIGHT!
HIMURA!
SO THIS...
...IS WHAT THIS VILLAGE HAS BECOME.
KEEN
UGH...
PWIK

SO THIS IS TO BE THE FUTURE OF JAPAN...
...IN THE NEW AGE SHISHIO BRINGS.

PEOPLE GOVERNED BY VIOLENCE, AND FEAR...
IF THIS VILLAGE DIES, IT'S YOUR FAULT!
TROMP TROMP
YOU MURDERERS!
THEIR ONE HOPE SIMPLY TO LIVE, FORGETTING WHAT LIFE IS FOR.

SAITŌ...
DID THE GOVERNMENT REALLY ABANDON THIS VILLAGE?
AND NOT JUST THIS ONE. TEN VILLAGES HAVE BEEN ABANDONED TO SHISHIO ALREADY.

THE POLICE NO LONGER EVEN PRETEND AT RECAPTURING THEM.

BUT WHY DON'T YOU CALL IN THE ARMY IF THE POLICE CAN'T DO IT?

FOOL. IT'S ONLY BEEN HALF A YEAR SINCE THE SEINAN WAR.

IF THE ARMY HAS TO NEUTRALIZE AN INTERNAL SQUABBLE AGAIN, IT WILL ONLY MAKE JAPAN'S INSTABILITY OBVIOUS TO FOREIGN POWERS.

WHAT KIND OF DUMB REASON IS THAT?!

READ THIS WAY

LOOK. SUPPOSE THE ARMY WOULD HELP US.
THE POLITICIANS COULD NEVER APPROVE IT.
WHY ?!

BECAUSE EVERY ONE OF THEM...
...IS AFRAID TO FOLLOW THE EXAMPLE OF ŌKUBO.

TRUE. THE ARMY COULD RETAKE THE VILLAGES...
...BUT ANYONE WHO APPROVED THE ACTION WOULD PAY.

THE DIFFICULTY OF PREVENTING ASSASSINATIONS WITHIN THE GOVERNMENT ...
...WELL, YOU KNOW ABOUT THAT.
GOVERNMENT LEADERS ARE, IN THE END, HUMAN.
THEY SAVE THEMSELVES... AND THEY WAIT FOR SOMEONE ELSE TO SOLVE THE PROBLEM.

READ THIS WAY

WHO IS THIS "SOMEONE ELSE"?!
WHO IS IT THAT'S GOING TO SAVE THIS VILLAGE?!

WHO IS... WHO...
...IS GOING TO AVENGE THIS BOY'S SORROWS?!

THE VILLAGE, THE POLICE...
...THE ARMY, THE GOVERN-MENT...
...ALL OF THEM WILL DO JUST AS SHISHIO MAKOTO PLEASES.

THAT IS WHY, NOW...
...HITOKIRI AND SHINSENGUMI *BOTH* ARE NEEDED.
WE KNOW THE LOCATION OF SHISHIO'S LAIR.
WE KNOW WHAT WE MUST DO.

YES.
CHK
WAIT! I'M COMING, TOO!
NO. YOU STAY HERE.
DM
NEVER! HOW CAN I FORGIVE ...
...ANYONE WHO DOES *THIS*?!
MISAO-DONO.
WHAT ?!
I DON'T CARE *WHAT* YOU SAY, I—
FP
COULD YOU PLEASE...
...STAY BY EIJI'S SIDE?

MY DEEPEST APOLOGIES, SIR!
AT THE CLIFFS OF HAKONE, HIMURA BATTŌSAI JUMPED INTO THE FOREST SO SUDDENLY THAT I LOST HIM.
BRR
BRR
WE'RE SEARCHING FOR HIM WITH EVERYONE WE HAVE, SO PLEASE...
WHAT SHALL WE DO, SHISHIO-SAN?

DON'T GROVEL. I FORGIVE YOU.

I TOOK MY FIRST MEDICINAL BATH IN *MONTHS* TODAY, AND I'M IN A FINE MOOD.

NOW GO FIND BATTŌSAI BEFORE I CHANGE MY MIND.

TH- THANK YOU SO MUCH!
PHEW
LUCKY YOU!

BUT THE NEXT TIME YOU FAIL US, I WILL NOT FORGIVE YOU.

SETA-SAMA!

WHAT'S WITH THE RACKET?

UM...

READ THIS WAY

PSST
...
PSST
HM...

SHISHIO-SAN, SHISHIO-SAN...!
HMPH. WHAT NOW?

ONE WITH A CROSS-SHAPED SCAR ON HIS CHEEK AND A POLICEMAN CARRYING A JAPANESE SWORD...
...WERE SEEN HEADING TOWARD THIS MANSION.

I SEE...
HE COMES TO ME BEFORE I CAN GREET HIM. A BOLD MAN.

SŌJIRŌ, WHY DON'T YOU GO AND MEET THEM?
SURE.

READ THIS WAY

ALSO...

...HAVE SENKAKU PREPARE FOR BATTLE.

DIG DIG DIG DIG

I'LL KILL YOU.

Rurouni
Kenshin

Act 68—A Portrait of the Ambitious

THAT VOICE...

BE CAREFUL, SAITŌ.
HE IS THE ONE WHO ASSAS-SINATED ŌKUBO.

NOW, REALLY. I'M JUST A GUIDE TODAY.
SEE? I CARRY NO WEAPONS.
WAVE
WAVE

SHISHIO-SAN AWAITS YOU IN THE BACK.

SHALL WE?

...

WE CAN'T MOVE FORWARD BY BEING CAREFUL.

LET'S GO.

Act 68—A Portrait of the Ambitious

SHISHIO-SAMA, WILL YOU HAVE A DRINK AFTER YOUR BATH?
SP
THEY'RE HERE.
OH.

SO YOU ARE...
...SHISHIO MAKOTO.

PLEASE! "SHISHIO MAKOTO-*KUN*," AT LEAST.
A VISITOR SHOULD HAVE BETTER MANNERS.

NOT THAT *YOUR* MANNERS HAVE BEEN MUCH BETTER.
HEY. SHOULD YOU BE STANDING AT EASE LIKE THAT?
BATTŌSAI COULD TAKE ONE LEAP AT SHISHIO AND KILL HIM.
I'M NOT WORRIED. HIMURA, UNLIKE *YOU*...
...WOULD *NEVER* RESORT TO DIRTY TRICKS.
HEH
TSK
HE SEES CLEARLY.

SHK

HEY, WAIT A MINUTE!

WHERE DO YOU PLAN TO GO WITH THAT?!

TP

TO SHISHIO'S MANSION.

I'M GOING TO AVENGE MY PARENTS.

WHAT ARE YOU TALKING ABOUT? YOU CAN'T DO THAT!

I'M ALONE NOW.

I HAVE NO FEAR FOR MY LIFE.

HOLD IT!

TM

WHY?! IF YOU PLAN TO STOP ME—
...IDIOT. SENKAKU ISN'T THE *ONLY* ONE AT SHISHIO'S MANSION!

THEIR BOSS IS THERE— SHISHIO. AND THOSE SOLDIERS. WITH THE MASKS!

MNG

YOU WON'T EVEN GET *PAST* THE GATE!

SO...
I'LL HELP YOU OUT.
HEH

I UNDERSTAND HOW YOU FEEL. IF I FOUND OUT *THEY* WERE DEAD...
...THE ONIWABANSHŪ... *NOTHING* WOULD STOP ME FROM AVENGING THEM!
TUG
I'M SORRY, HIMURA...BUT I'M GOING TO HELP HIM!
I DON'T CARE IF YOU COME, JUST DON'T SLOW ME DOWN.
HSST
YARGH!
WHY DID YOU TARGET THIS PLACE?
YOUR GOAL IS THIS NATION ITSELF...
...NOT ONE OR TWO SMALL VILLAGES.

READ THIS WAY

ONSEN.

THE HOT SPRINGS HERE SOOTHE MY BURNT SKIN...

...BUT IF OTHER CUSTOMERS SAW ME, THEY'D BE SCARED. SO I MADE IT MINE.

YOU...

...DESTROYED THE VILLAGE FOR *THAT*...?

PLEASE. I'M JOKING.

TEE HEE

HOO HOO HOO...

DON'T GET SO WORKED UP.

YOU'RE AS HUMORLESS AS THEY SAY YOU ARE.

THAT WAS A CHEAP TAUNT.

GONG

DON'T GET HYSTERICAL, LIKE THAT WEASEL GIRL.

A-CHOO

?

SNOO...

I TOOK THIS VILLAGE AS A STRONGHOLD FROM WHICH TO CONQUER THE EASTERN SHORE.
TP
AND I DO LIKE THE ONSEN HERE.
SHISHIO—
—SHUT UP.
GNG
SO, YOU SIT HERE IN YOUR *BANDAGES*, AND PLAN YOUR *REVENGE* AGAINST THE MEIJI GOVERNMENT.

...CAPTAIN OF THE 3RD SHINSENGUMI UNIT, SAITŌ HAJIME.

I THOUGHT YOU WERE MORE OF *MY* MIND THAN THAT OF BATTŌSAI, SO I EXPECTED YOU TO UNDERSTAND A BIT BETTER...BUT, NOT QUITE.

I HAVE NO DESIRE TO TAKE REVENGE ON THOSE WHO GAVE ME THESE WOUNDS.

IN FACT, I THANK THEM FOR IT. THESE WOUNDS BURNED MANY LESSONS INTO MY BODY.
KRAK
"TRUST, AND BE BETRAYED."
"RELAX YOUR GUARD, AND BE KILLED."
"KILL BEFORE YOU ARE KILLED."

AND ALSO...
"WOMEN WILL COME TO A REAL MAN NO MATTER WHAT HE LOOKS LIKE."

IS THAT SO? THEN SHOULDN'T YOU BE MORE CONTENT?
IT'S *TIRING* TO HAVE TO RUN AROUND THE COUNTRY AFTER YOU.
NNN
SIGH
YOU AND I AND BATTŌSAI HERE WERE ALL MEN WHO LIVED THROUGH THE BAKUMATSU.
WHY CAN'T YOU UNDER-STAND MY FEELINGS?

THE EMPEROR, THE SHŌGUN, THE EXCLUSION OF FOREIGNERS, THE OPENING OF THE PORTS...

...BAKUMATSU WAS THE FIRST ERA OF *CHAOS* IN 30 YEARS.

"THE EMPEROR, THE GOVERNMENT, SATSUMA, CHŌSHŪ, OR TOSA.

"...ALL CARRIED THEIR BANNERS OF 'RIGHT' THROUGH ENDLESS KILLING."

A MAN FORGED IN SUCH AN AGE...

...MUST BE A MAN OF UNQUENCHABLE AMBITION.

CLAP
CLAP

...

BUT BY THE TIME MY WOUNDS HEALED...
...THERE WAS SOMETHING CALLED THE *MEIJI* *GOVERNMENT*.
TWIRL
PAP

A GOVERNMENT THAT FEARS TO SEND AN *ARMY* TO FINISH OFF A HALF-DEAD BEING LIKE ME, BECAUSE IT FEARS THE *EYES* OF FOREIGN COUNTRIES.
A GOVERNMENT OF ***WEAKLINGS.***

I CAN'T LEAVE THIS NATION TO A GOVERNMENT LIKE THAT!

SO!
KRAAK

IF THE REVOLUTION IS OVER...

...THEN I'LL START *ANOTHER* ONE! THIS TIME I WILL GAIN *CONTROL*!

THEN I *WILL* MAKE THE COUNTRY STRONGER!

HEH

THAT IS THE "RIGHT" I BRING JAPAN.

BUT...

...IT'S NOT *YOU* WHO BLEEDS FOR YOUR "RIGHT."

THE ONES WHO BLEED...
...ARE THOSE WHO LIVE PEACEFULLY IN THIS AGE.

IT IS THE FITTEST WHO SURVIVE IN THIS WORLD.
BUT I WON'T ASK YOU TO UNDER-STAND THAT.

SHISHIO MAKOTO...
NO ONE ELSE MAY BE ALLOWED TO BLEED...
...FOR YOUR PERSONAL "RIGHT."
SAITŌ-SAN...
...HOW ABOUT YOU?
I DON'T MAKE A HABIT OF SPEECHES LIKE HIS...
...BUT MY SWORD TURNS AGAINST YOU, TOO.
I HAVE NO OBJECTION TO FIGHTING YOU...
...BUT, IF WE ARE TO DO IT, I'D RATHER IT BE IN KYOTO.
NO...?
WELL, IF FIGHT WE MUST...
THUMP

GRM
!
...LET'S LEAVE IT TO THE MAN...
...WHO CONTROLS THIS VILLAGE... SENKAKU!!!

SO YOU ARE SENKAKU ...
...THE MAN WHO KILLED EIJI'S BROTHER AND PARENTS.
HWAAH !!!

HE'S QUICK.
HYOO
HYOO
YOU'RE SLOW!
!!

I WILL TAKE YOU DOWN BEFORE SHISHIO!!

The Secret Life of Characters (24)

—Shishio Makoto—

Ideally not a character who should be appearing in this space just yet, there've been enough questions about him that I'll give you a taste—but not too much of a taste.

Shishio was born of my editor's urging to "do a big story," and therefore has no model in terms of personality. I originally thought of him as a man out for revenge, since that would make it easier for me to express his grief concerning the government, but that made the story smaller in scale. Therefore, I decided that he would enjoy *at the same time* revenge and conquering, thereby making him a destructive being—kind of like Serizawa Kamo of the Shinsengumi. I also think there may be some influence from the maliciousness of *ShinSamurai Spirits*' "Kibagami Genjūrō."

I've heard a few theories as to what might be visual models, but actually it's "Aonuma Shizuma" of *Inugami Ke no Ichizoku* (The Inugami Family). I saw this movie as a child and was very influenced by it, so when it was decided Shishio would be burned over most of his body, I thought of a character wearing a rubber, human mask like Shizuma. That, though, would have made drawing expressions difficult—not to mention the difficulty of making rubber seem realistic in black and white. Additionally, the sheer agony of his condition wouldn't have been conveyed by it, so we settled on the figure we have today—all wrapped in bandages—except being wrapped up in bandages wouldn't look exciting—so we crisscrossed the bandages on his face, gave him some weird headgear, and otherwise fancied it up. How does it look...? I also wanted him to be cool, like Kibagami, so I gave him a scratchy-looking robe, a pipe, an umbrella, a folding screen... and a sexy companion. This is off-topic, but Shishio showing up just once during a Bakumatsu scene is totally Kibagami (I didn't think I needed a pre-burn design for him, so didn't have one). To those of you who saw that and maybe got upset, my apologies.

Act 69
The Tactics of Battle

TAKE DOWN?
ME?
YOU.
TRY IT!!

SENKAKU, WHO TO THIS DAY HAS CARVED UP 99 PEOPLE...
...WILL MAKE YOU HIS 100TH!!!
DG DG DG DG
ONLY 99?
HEH
AND HERE I THOUGHT YOU WERE A WARRIOR!
!
OH!
"SHIN-SOKU"—THE FAMOUS "GOD SPEED"!

SENKAKU NEVER LOSES IN SPEED.
HSS!
BEHIND ME, BATTOSAI !!
!!
NNNNN

READ
THIS
WAY

HEH. IS BATTŌSAI A COWARD WHOSE ONLY SKILL IS TO STRIKE FROM BEHIND?
THAT'S SOMETHING ...
VYOO

...IT'S NOTHING TO BE PROUD OF.

YOUR SPEED MATCHES MINE!
BUT I HAVE SHEER STRENGTH YOU DON'T...

...I CAN DO, TOO.

...AND THESE KNUCKLE BLADES TAKE FULL ADVANTAGE OF BOTH!

READ THIS WAY
DM DM DM
VWAAAH!
I HEARD TODAY'S INTRUDERS ARE QUITE ADEPT...
NOBODY CAN WITHSTAND MASTER SENKAKU'S "MINCING BLOW."
THERE'S NO NEED FOR US THIS TIME.
LET'S TAKE IT EASY.
ON THE CONTRARY...
...YOU'RE NEEDED RIGHT NOW.
!
WHO ARE YOU?!

MAKIMACHI MISAO...

...NEED GIVE HER NAME TO NO VILLAIN!

...YOU JUST DID.

AGH!

SHOOT!!

—NEVER MIND THAT! YOU'D ALL BETTER GET OUT OF THE WAY OR YOU'LL BE SORRY!

YAH!

!

"OR YOU'LL BE SOR-R-RY!" SHEESH!

YOU BRAINLESS WENCH!

I AM NOT!

HWUH!

KK

ZIP

DOM
DOM
HYOO!

YOU... RUNNING HERE TO THERE, THERE TO HERE.

YOU AND I ARE AT THE SAME SPEED!

ZZZ

DO YOU THINK YOU CAN KEEP RUNNING LIKE A COCKROACH FOREVER ?!

VMM

WK

BWOK

HIMURA IS HAVING A HARD TIME...

HE'S BEEN PUSHED AROUND AND HASN'T HAD A CHANCE TO STRIKE, NOT EVEN ONCE.

WHY DON'T YOU...
...HELP HIM OUT?
YOU'RE JOKING.
I DON'T PLAN ON REVEALING MY SWORD MOVES ON AN OPPONENT LIKE *THAT*.
LOOK.
JAB

READ THIS WAY

EVEN WHILE HE WAS JUST SMIRKING AND SPEAKING FREELY...

...ONCE THE BATTLE STARTED, HIS EYES CHANGED.

HE'S TRYING TO ANALYZE EVERY MOVE BATTŌSAI MAKES.
HE IS RECKLESS, BUT HE HASN'T LET HIS GUARD DOWN.

BATTŌSAI OF COURSE CAN FEEL HIS EYES...
...AND *THAT* IS WHY HE IS WAITING FOR HIS OPPONENT'S SELF-DESTRUCTION.

"SELF-DESTRUCTION"?

IT'S ABOUT TIME.
WILL YOU...
HYOO
...GIVE UP THIS...
!

DMMM
GUAAAAH?!
BMIK
BMIK
MY...LEG IS BROKEN...
NONSENSE! WE WERE MOVING AT THE SAME SPEED! HOW CAN MY BODY HAVE HIT ITS LIMIT...
...BEFORE YOUR PUNY BODY HIT ITS?!
BY MOVING REPETITIVELY WITHOUT DROPPING YOUR SPEED...
WE MOVED AT THE SAME SPEED, BUT YOUR BODY IS HEAVIER...
...SO THE BURDEN ON IT WAS GREATER.
...YOU'VE EXCEEDED THE IMPACT YOUR BODY COULD STAND.

READ THIS WAY

NO, THAT CAN'T BE! THAT'S NEVER HAPPENED BEFORE!
MY BODY SHOULDN'T HIT THE LIMIT AT SUCH A SPEED—
FOOL, DON'T YOU SEE YET?
BATTŌSAI SLIGHTLY INCREASED HIS SPEED EVERY TIME HE MOVED.
YOU BELIEVED YOU WERE MOVING AT THE SAME SPEED AND FELL FOR IT.

YOU WERE SAYING YOU'VE KILLED 99 PEOPLE, BUT...
HEH
...YOUR 100TH KILL SEEMS TO BE YOU.

...
WELL.
YOU THINK SO MANY THINGS WHILE YOU'RE FIGHTING.
TP
!

IT... WAS A LIE...
I DIDN'T KILL THAT MANY PEOPLE!
NINETY-NINE WAS JUST A FIGURE OF EXPRESSION... YOU SEE?
BUT YOU *WERE* THE ONE WHO KILLED EIJI'S FAMILY, WEREN'T YOU?
SENKAKU.
I DIDN'T REALLY EXPECT YOU TO WIN, BUT...
...IF YOU LOSE WITHOUT MAKING BATTŌSAI REVEAL A SINGLE MOVE...
...I'LL PERSONALLY...
...PUT AN *END* TO YOU.

PWIK
...
U...
U... UUU...
SHAKE
SHAKE
SHAKE
UVAAAAAH !!

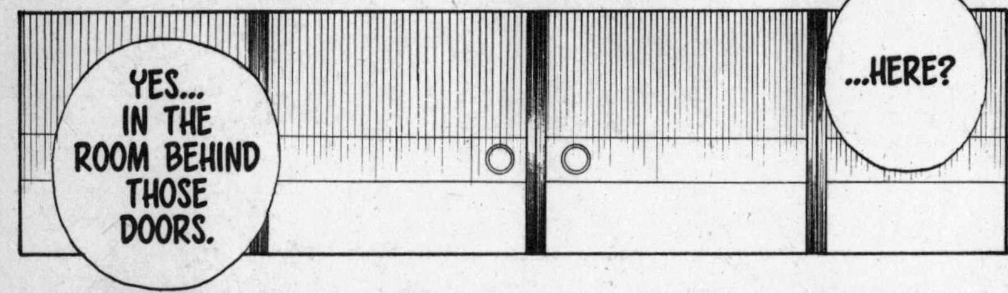

...HERE?
YES... IN THE ROOM BEHIND THOSE DOORS.

THANKS.
'NIGHT, THEN.
OWW.
NOW... WE DON'T WANT TO BE CAUGHT.
QUIETLY, QUIETLY.
SSS

HITEN MITSURUGI-RYŪ...
!!
...RYŪSHŌSEN!

READ THIS WAY
IDIOT... TAKING PITY ON THAT MUSCLE-HEAD...
THAT KINDNESS MAY COST YOU YOUR LIFE.
TCH
TP
IT DOESN'T MATTER.
TM
I'M NOT SO WORRIED ABOUT THIS ONE...
...
WOW

The Secret Life of Characters (25)

—Senkaku—

To be honest, Senkaku was *supposed* to be the first of the "Ten Swords," so Watsuki went to a great deal of trouble in creating him. But then there were Sōjirō and Shishio—and Kenshin and the others needed to get to Kyoto—so Senkaku became a violent village despot.

At first the kind of character who could only yell "Gaaaah" or "Guaaah" or things like that, Senkaku was an experiment—I'd never done an antagonist who didn't speak. One editor's comment during a meeting, though ("He's not a wild animal"), quickly changed *that.* No model in terms of his personality, then; after the change, Senkaku was pretty much just muscle-head small fry.

Senkaku's design originated during the designing of the four Abukuma priests. Created for defeat, I had no particular attachment to the four priests, but I *was* somewhat interested in how well I might be able to draw the different, bald heads. One was a cone-head, and I thought: *What a waste for an unimportant character.* So I used it for Senkaku, instead (though he turned out to be an unimportant character, too...). When I think back, probably I was influenced by the Coneheads in the Sega Saturn commercial, and by the Giant Soldier in *Nausicaä*. I still have my regrets about him; within my group of friends, he's known as the "sexy dynamite" of *Rurouni Kenshin* ("especially," they say, "in the groin area"). Very popular, needless to say. What I most regret is not being able to use his *hissatsu-waza* special technique, "Piercing Head-Butt."

Act 70
The Sword of Heaven

BAMM

...GET YOUR SWORD...

...SHISHIO MAKOTO.

I DON'T KNOW WHAT'S GOING ON, BUT IT LOOKS SERIOUS.
THIS...ISN'T ANYTHING WE SHOULD STICK OUR NOSES IN.
KLATTA
SO STOP SNEAKING AROUND... AND WATCH.

BOMP!
JUST DON'T LEAVE MY SIDE.
MISAO-DONO!
!
THAT MOVE CALLED RYŪSHŌSEN...
YOU SWUNG UPWARD ONTO SENKAKU'S CHIN, BUT...
...IT'S ORIGINALLY A MOVE DESIGNED FOR A BLADE, YES?

I'D HEARD FROM MY MEN THAT YOU HAD QUIT BEING HITOKIRI AND BECOME RUROUNI...
...BUT I COULDN'T BELIEVE IT, NOT TILL I SAW WITH MY OWN EYES.

TO TRY AND BEAT *ME* LIKE THAT...

...YOU HAVEN'T A CHANCE IN *HELL*.

AND I DON'T *LIKE* BORING FIGHTS.
SNAP
ZIP
PLOP
PLOP
PLOP

I'LL WAIT FOR YOU IN KYOTO...

...SO COME BACK ONCE YOU'RE HITOKIRI AGAIN.

RUNNING WITH YOUR TAIL TUCKED BETWEEN YOUR LEGS?

AH!

READ THIS WAY

FWUMP
SŌJIRŌ, AMUSE YOURSELF WITH THEM IN MY STEAD.
OH, MAY I?
GRIP
YES. IN RETURN FOR THE "RYŪSHŌSEN"...
...SHOW THEM YOUR "TENKEN."

ZAH
I SHAN'T HOLD BACK.
HEY HIMURA! WHAT ARE YOU DOZING OFF FOR?!
IF YOU DON'T HURRY, THE BANDAGE MAN IS GONNA GET AWAY!

DWN
RRR
RRR
RRR
RRR
!
WH...
?
WHAT WAS THAT?!
FUMP
DIRECTING KI TOWARD HIM IS LIKE PUSHING ONE'S SELF OFF AGAINST A CURTAIN.
I'VE BEEN DOING IT MYSELF FOR A WHILE.

CLOP
CLOP
CLOP
CLOP
SHISHIO-SAMA.
HM.
WHAT IS THIS "TENKEN" YOU SPOKE OF?
THAT'S HIS NAME.
A *SWORD* WIELDED BY HEAVENLY *SKILL*.
HE IS HEAVEN'S SWORD.
BUT THEN... ISN'T BATTŌSAI THE SAME?
PERHAPS, BUT...
...SŌJIRŌ, DUE TO THE FAMILY SITUATION IN WHICH HE GREW UP...
...NOW LACKS ALL EMOTIONS BUT *RAKU*—"COMFORT."
THAT MAN LACKS NOT ONLY BATTLE *KI*...
...BUT AGGRESSION, AND RAGE.

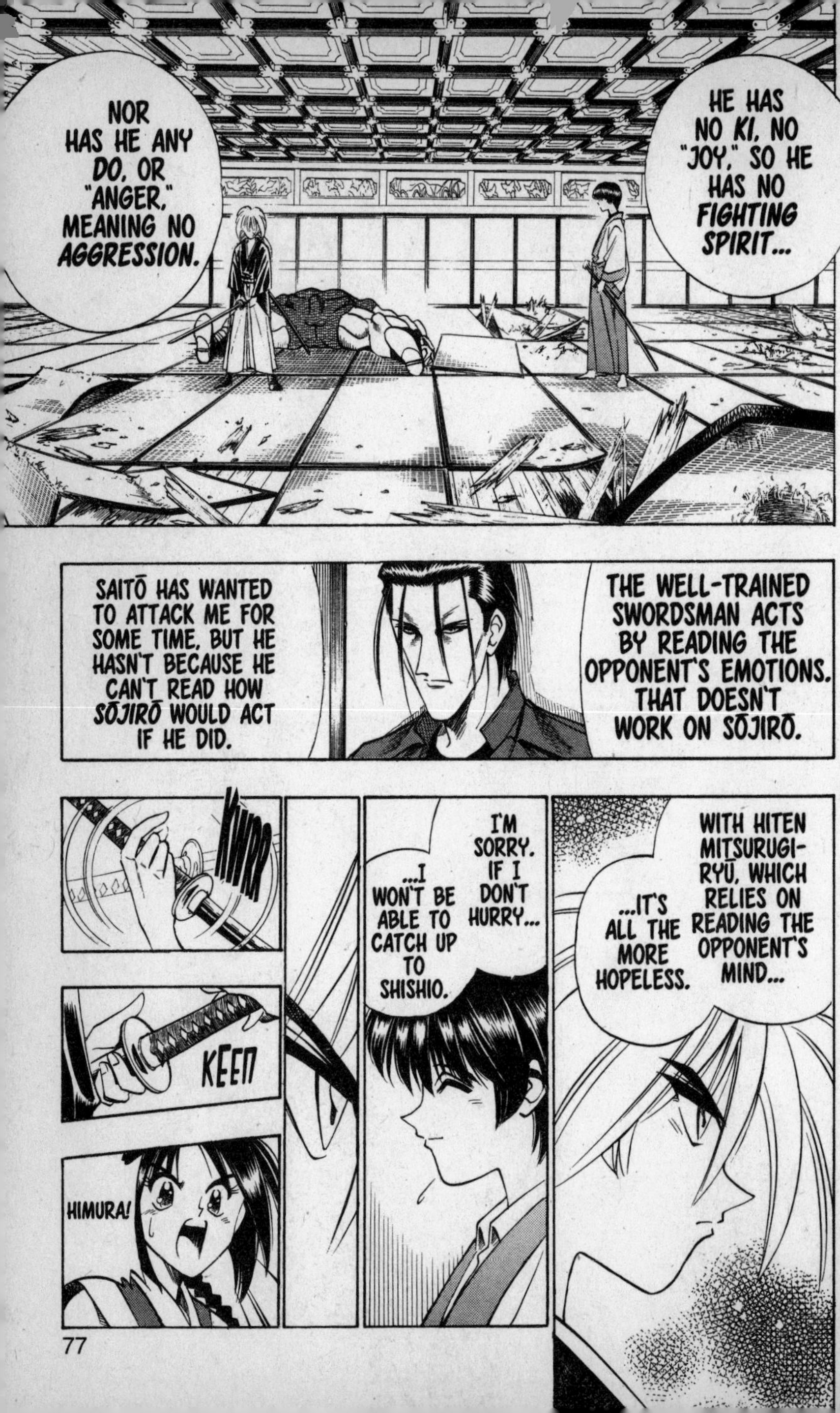

HE HAS NO *KI*, NO "JOY," SO HE HAS NO *FIGHTING SPIRIT*...

NOR HAS HE ANY *DO*, OR "ANGER," MEANING NO *AGGRESSION*.

THE WELL-TRAINED SWORDSMAN ACTS BY READING THE OPPONENT'S EMOTIONS. THAT DOESN'T WORK ON SŌJIRŌ.

SAITŌ HAS WANTED TO ATTACK ME FOR SOME TIME, BUT HE HASN'T BECAUSE HE CAN'T READ HOW *SŌJIRŌ* WOULD ACT IF HE DID.

WITH HITEN MITSURUGI-RYŪ, WHICH RELIES ON READING THE OPPONENT'S MIND...

...IT'S ALL THE MORE HOPELESS.

I'M SORRY. IF I DON'T HURRY...

...I WON'T BE ABLE TO CATCH UP TO SHISHIO.

KWRR

KEEN

HIMURA!

ZAH
!
...I THOUGHT SO.
IF HE CAN'T REACT TO THE OPPONENT...
...THEN IT'S MOST ADVANTAGEOUS TO STRIKE WITH THE FASTEST SWORD.
BATTŌ-JUTSU...
...OF COURSE.
THEN...
...I, TOO...
ZAH

JJ...
JJ...
CHK...
CHK...

THEN THE MATCH WILL BE...
...BATTŌ-JUTSU.
AND THEIR SWORD SPEED...

...IS
EQUAL
!!

HOWEVER...

BETWEEN BATTŌSAI, WHO HAS *SWORN OFF* KILLING OTHERS, AND SŌJIRŌ...
...WHO KNOWS NO *AI*, NO "SORROW," AND THINKS *NOTHING* OF KILLING...
...THE SAME "SWORD OF HEAVEN"...
...IS A VERY DIFFERENT WEAPON!
UNLESS HE IS *WILLING* TO *KILL*...
...BATTŌSAI WILL *NEVER* BEAT SŌJIRŌ.
MATCH OVER...
...YOU THINK?
YEAH.
IT'S A DRAW...
...BOTH OF YOU, UNABLE TO CONTINUE.

!
HOOO!
YOU GO, HIMURA!
ASTOUND-ING...
IT'S BEYOND REPAIR.
AH, WELL.
CHING
IT'S SHISHIO'S ANYWAY.
THERE IS NO WINNER OR LOSER IN THIS MATCH.
TP
I'LL BE ON MY WAY FOR TODAY. BUT I HOPE WE MEET AGAIN.

READ THIS WAY

BEFORE THEN...

...PLEASE FIND ANOTHER SWORD.

TUMP

TUMP

The Secret Life of Characters (26)
—Seta Sōjirō—

Like Shishio, this character shouldn't be showing up in here just yet either, but I'll again give you another taste, since so many have asked.

Personality-wise, Sōjirō's model is Okita Sōshi, captain of the Shinsengumi first unit. The name "Seta Sōjirō" comes from "Okita Sōjirō"—Sōshi's name earlier in life. Since the name is the same, some readers have sought a connection between Okita and Sōjirō—but, let me just put this out there—there isn't one. Okita is just Seta's model.

Okita Sōshi is so famous there's no need to speak of him here—there's always a variety of books about him at the stores, if you're curious. He's so popular that, during the first "*RuroKen*" popularity poll, he ranked seventh... even though he'd only appeared in a few panels! Watsuki has used Okita as portrayed by [well-known historical novelist] Shiba Ryōtarō, but (this time) it's not the Okita of Shiba's "*Moeyo Ken* (Burn, O Sword)," but the Okita of "*Shinsengumi Keppūroku* (Record of Shinsengumi Bloodshed)" he's using... and *that* Okita has lost an important part of his human heart, making him emotionless and pretty scary. Some Shinsengumi fans are upset that a character modeled upon Okita is appearing as a villain, but since it's the "*Keppūroku*" Okita that's the model, I believe it works well, and helps to make Seta a strong antagonist.

Seta is more difficult to draw than first thought. As of present, I've only done about 1/4th of what I've imagined in my mind. I do want to do him justice, as he is such a popular character, but....

Design-wise, there's no real model. Okita was always envisioned by me with the bangs, and so when he came out looking like this, it was no surprise. I also gave him a slightly feminized air... so that a smile would look good on him.

Act 71—To Kyoto, Once More

HIS SAKABATŌ...

...BROKE?

SHISHIO AND HIS GANG GOT AWAY AS WELL.

HSS

HEY.

WELL, WE CAN MAKE ANOTHER SWORD...

...AND WE CAN CHASE SHISHIO AGAIN.

WE WERE AT LEAST ABLE TO RID THIS VILLAGE OF SHISHIO'S MEN.

THAT ITSELF IS ENOUGH.

Act 71
To Kyoto, Once More

READ
THIS
WAY

SS

PWIK
PWIK
PWIK
HOOOH
HOOOH

HE'S BREATHING...
HE'S NOT DEAD.

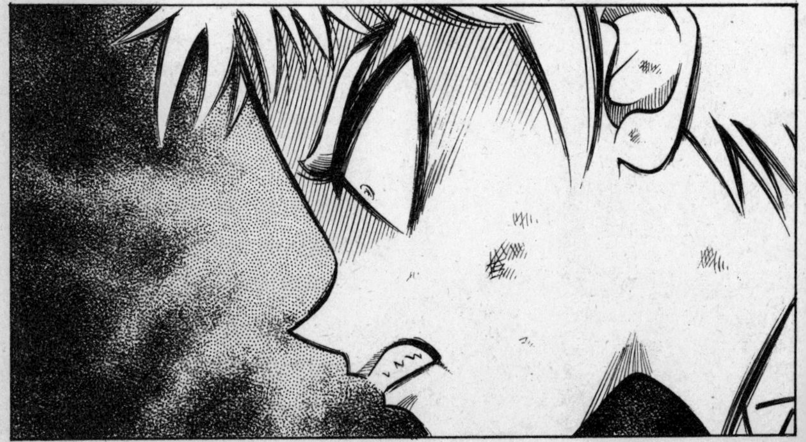

Clang!
EIJI.
DIE, SENKAKU!
HEY, STOP. HE'S ALREADY—
!

READ THIS WAY
GAP
!
NG
UWAH!

HE'S NO USE TO US DEAD.
THERE'S STILL TOO MUCH WE NEED OF HIM.
THIS IS MY REVENGE! DON'T STOP ME!
IDIOT.
REVENGE KILLINGS WERE OUTLAWED IN THE SIXTH YEAR OF MEIJI.
I'VE ENOUGH TO DO ALREADY.

BESIDES, IF HE'S TURNED OVER TO THE LAW...
...HE'LL BE TORTURED AND THEN EXECUTED.
GONG

READ THIS WAY
IT'S MUCH CRUELER THAN KILLING HIM WHILE HE'S UN-CONSCIOUS.
HEH
OGRE...

SHUT UP!
I DON'T CARE ABOUT LAWS OR EXECUTIONS!

IF I DON'T TAKE REVENGE WITH MY VERY OWN HANDS...

...HOW CAN MY *FAMILY* EVER—?

WHAT THE DEAD WISH FOR IS NOT REVENGE...
...BUT HAPPINESS FOR THOSE LEFT ALIVE.
IF YOU DIRTY YOUR HANDS NOW...
...NO ONE WILL BE HAPPY.

AS TIME PASSES, THIS SMALL HAND WILL GROW LARGER...
DON'T GROW INTO A MAN LIKE SHISHIO OR SENKAKU, OPPRESSING OTHERS WITH POWER.
...AND YOU WILL BECOME AN ADULT.
DON'T GROW INTO A MAN LIKE THESE VILLAGERS, PARALYZED BY FEAR.
GROW INTO A MAN LIKE YOUR BROTHER, WHO WANTED, AT THE END, FOR YOU TO BE SAFE.
...AND TO ACHIEVE HAPPINESS.

KSHANG
FOR NOW, AT LEAST...
...I GUESS IT'S SETTLED.
HERE'S A FACE CLOTH.
WIPE YOUR TEARS.
WHY, YOU ...!
SCHNOFFF
SO, "IT'S SETTLED" ...
...IS IT?

I'M NOT AT FAULT.
IF YOU'RE GOING TO GET MAD, GET MAD AT HIMURA.
SCRATCH SCRATCH
DESTROYING THE "NAGASONE KOTETSU" WITH A SAKABATŌ.
I'VE UNDER-ESTIMATED HIM.
KOTETSU?
YOU'VE GREAT SKILLS, BUT YOU'RE IGNOR-ANT.
"KOTETSU" IS ONE OF THE 31 GREATEST SMITHS. ANY SWORDSMAN WOULD KILL TO POSSESS IT IF HE COULD.
?
SŌJIRŌ, I'VE A REQUEST FOR YOU.
IF IT'S NOT ABOUT PAYING YOU BACK, GO AHEAD.
CONTACT EACH OF THE "TEN SWORDS"...
...AND TELL THEM TO GATHER AT KYOTO.
!!

I WANT TO PRY OUT THE "HITOKIRI BATTŌSAI"...

...TRAPPED WITHIN "HIMURA KENSHIN" EVEN IF I HAVE TO DO IT BY FORCE.

HEH

HYOOOOOOOO

NOW...

...SHINGETSU VILLAGE CAN RETURN TO NORMAL.

YAY

WAAH

RAH

YAY

RAH

YAY

EVERYONE *CHEERING* LIKE THAT...
I DON'T FEEL *RIGHT* ABOUT THIS.

IT'S ONLY THE BEGINNING. THE UGLINESS OF THEIR SOULS WAS EXPOSED WITH THIS INCIDENT...
...MEANING, IT'LL BE *ROUGH* FOR A WHILE.
I DON'T FEEL "RIGHT" ABOUT *YOU*, EITHER.
THIS VILLAGE IS STILL MY HOME-LAND...
...I'LL PRAY FOR THE BEST.

NOW...
IT'S TIME FOR ME TO GO BACK.
ALL RIGHT, BUT...
...WHAT'S TO BE DONE WITH EIJI?

NEITHER YOU NOR I CAN TAKE HIM ALONG...
...SO I'LL HAVE *TOKIO* TAKE CARE OF HIM UNTIL THINGS SETTLE DOWN.
"TOKIO"?

MY WIFE.
DOOOOM

W-W-W-WIFE?!
YOU'RE *MARRIED*?
NDEED HE IS.

DON'T WORRY. TOKIO IS A GOOD WOMAN.
SHE'LL TAKE GOOD CARE OF EIJI.
SHE MUST BE *SOMETHING*... IF SHE CAN BE *THIS* GUY'S WIFE.
TOKIO
ARTIST'S SKETCH
...A VERITABLE BODHISATTVA.

DON'T WORRY ABOUT US.
TM
TM
YOU JUST HURRY TO KYOTO...

...AND RETURN TO BEING HITOKIRI.

THIS BATTLE MUST HAVE MADE IT CLEAR. AS RUROUNI, YOU CAN'T DEFEAT SHISHIO...

...OR EVEN HIS CLOSE COHORTS.

IT WAS A GOOD TIME FOR YOUR SAKABATŌ TO BREAK.
QUIT DITHERING AND MAKE THE DECISION.
I'M COUNTING ON YOU...
...COUNTING ON YOUR PAST.
HIMURA.

HMMM
O-OKAY, SO MAYBE I DON'T GET IT...
...BUT THEY RAN, AND WE WON...
GLINT
...SO IGNORE WHAT SAITŌ SAYS... HE DIDN'T DO ANYTHING ANYWAY!
SO TURN THAT FROWN UPSIDE DOWN, HUH?!
HIMURA, YOU LOOK IMPRESSIVE WHEN YOU'RE GRIM AND SILENT...
...BUT YOU'RE KIND OF SCARY, TOO.
LOOK! SPECIAL ABILITY: "GIRL OF 100 FACES"!
I PREFER THE HIMURA WHO'S RELAXED AND SAYS "ORO."
ORO
...OHH, YEAH. HE'S MUCH BETTER.
RYŪSHŌSEN
WHAT MISAO-DONO LIKES IS NOT OF CONCERN.
OH...
WELL, IN THAT CASE...
—HEY.
YOU DON'T HAVE TO BE RUDE!

WE'VE SPENT A LOT OF TIME HERE...
...LET'S HURRY ON OUR WAY.
SHISHIO'S MEN PROBABLY WON'T ATTACK UNTIL KYOTO...
...SO LET'S TAKE THE EAST SEA ROAD.
ZT
ZT
...HE WAS...
...FOOLING WITH ME...!
MONSTER BIRD KICK OF RAGE!
BOOOT
KEEEE
LET'S JUST GET TO KYOTO BEFORE...
ORO.

MUST THIS ONE BECOME HITOKIRI ONCE MORE...?
THE ANSWER... LIES IN KYOTO.

AND...

RRG. I THINK I'M ACTUALLY LOST NOW.

WHICH WAY TO KYOTO, AGAIN...?

BLAST IT.

The Secret Life of Characters (27)

—Mishima Eiji—

The "Shingetsu Village" episode was meant to suggest a miniature version of Japan under Shishio's rule—i.e., as having a dark atmosphere. It was also a very offbeat "*RuroKen*" plotline. Between the tragedy of the story, and as the symbol of a new beginning, Eiji was born. Reading back now, I regret how he's pulled around by the plot and doesn't have much room for development as a character. Eiji's central theme is "revenge"—a theme huge to the entire series. Already in the near future there's another episode planned with "revenge" as its main theme. Of course, it'll come *after* the Kyoto story arc....

Another thing I'd hoped to portray with this episode was the ugly "village mentality" distinct to Japanese culture, but it didn't end up working out well. It seems it's difficult, portraying such a dark thing in adventure manga.

There's no model in terms of Eiji's design; I was short on time when I created him (I never seem to have enough time as of late), and had been doing a slightly long-haired young man, but since he didn't look like a village boy, I whited him out and drew him over, resulting in the finished version. (In his first, weekly magazine appearance—when he's being held by his nearly dead brother—you can see the earlier design. I fixed him for the graphic novel version you're reading now, though.)

There was no time for his costume, either, so I asked an assistant to "put some kind of pattern on the shirt, and tone on the pants," and that's how it turned out. The costume does maybe look a little too similar to Yahiko's... Cutting corners is never good. I should do this stuff myself, no matter *how* busy I am.

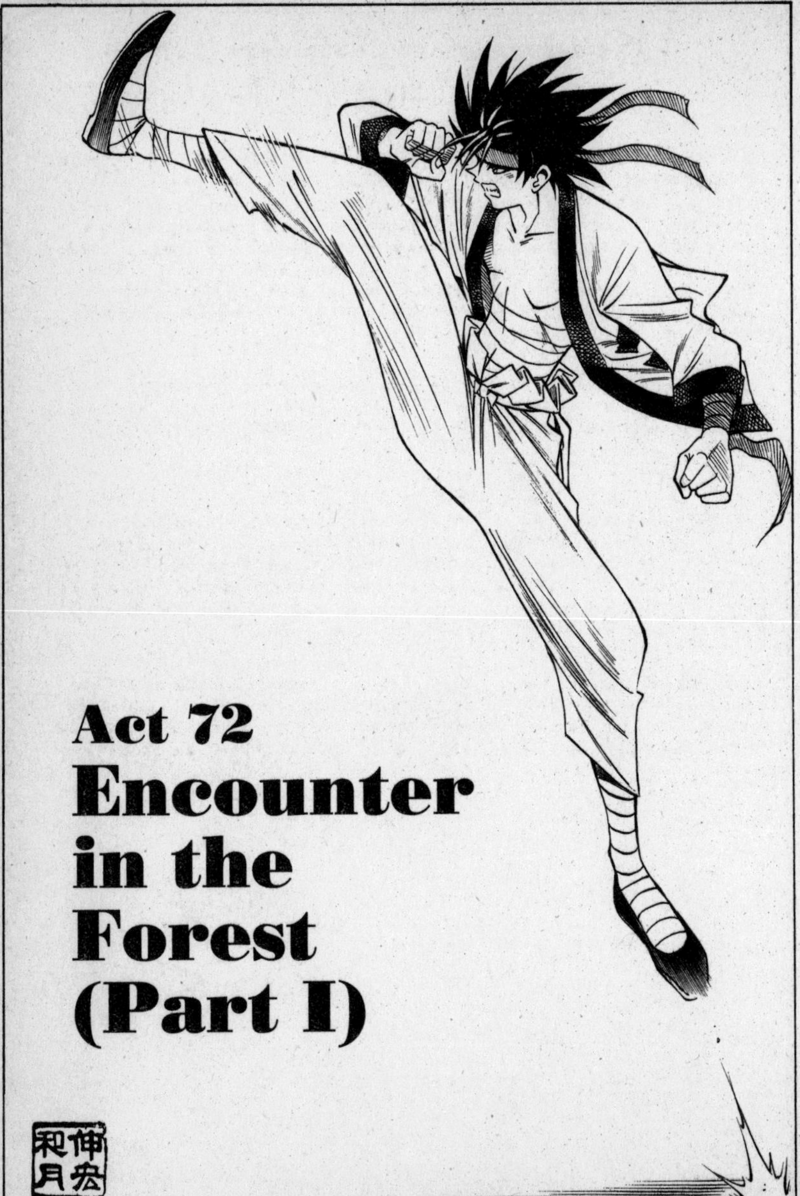

Act 72
Encounter in the Forest (Part I)

BLAST IT. WHICH WAY TO KYOTO, AGAIN?
MORE PRESSING—WHERE IN HELL IS *THIS?!*
HAS KENSHIN...
...REACHED KYOTO YET?
ARE YAHIKO AND KAORU ON THEIR WAY?
WHAT ABOUT MEGUMI? ...NO, SHE HAS HER PATIENTS.
HMPH.

READ THIS WAY

HE HAD BETTER NOT BE IN KYOTO...!
MMG

STRANGE...
...THIS FOREST LOOKS FAMILIAR...
...OR AM I JUST IMAGINING IT?

GROWWWL
FEH. THINKING OF HIM MAKES ME HUNGRY.
ROWL
THE LAST ONE.
AFTER THIS, I'LL HAVE TO CATCH *FROGS* OR SOMETHING.
OH, WELL.
HYOOO
POP

SSHHH
!
...
BUP
!

READ THIS WAY

SBOOP
BOING
HEY.
CHEW CHEW
WHAT MORON RUINED MY DINNER ?!
ZZZZZZZZZZZZZZZZ
ZAP!

煩苦餓鬼
飢餓苦畜生
逼迫苦黃泉

煩苦餓鬼
飢餓苦畜生
逼迫苦黃泉

OHN!
NG

...

OHN!

SOME MONK FROM SOME RELIGION...

...BUT WHAT TH' HECK'S HE DOING?

PRAYING FOR CROPS?

煩苦餓鬼
飢餓苦
畜生遍迫

ZAP

!
...HUH.

ZK...
ZUFF
THAT WAS... SOMETHING.

POWERS BORROWED FROM THE BUDDHA BY AN ADEPT PRIEST...
HEH
..."HŌRIKI," RIGHT? FIRST I'VE EVER SEEN 'EM USED.

ARE YOU LOST?
Tp
CH-KEEN
YEAH. MIND SHOWING ME THE WAY?

AN' IF YOU GOT ANY FOOD, CAN I HAVE IT?
FIRST TIME AT BEGGING, IS IT?

...AH, NOW I SEE. "DIRT DUMPLINGS," BECAUSE OF ME.
SORRY ABOUT THAT.
KRAKL
KRAKL
DON'T BE. YOUR TRAINING'S GOT ME A HOT MEAL.
HA
HA
PLUS, I GOT TO SEE HŌRIKI IN ACTION.
THOSE WERE *NOT* BUDDHIST POWERS.
HŌRIKI ARE ONLY A LIE INVENTED TO TRICK PEOPLE INTO BELIEVING.
EVEN I, AN ADEPT ON THE PATH OF BUDDHISM, HAVE NEVER SEEN THEM.
AND EVEN IF THERE *WERE* SUCH THINGS...
...THEY'RE NOTHING I WOULD BE ABLE TO USE NOW.
GMP

THEN YOU'RE...
...A FALLEN PRIEST?
FALLEN PRIEST
A DISGRACED OR CORRUPTED PRIEST WHO FEELS NO SHAME IN VIOLATING THE DIRECTIVES OF THE BUDDHA.
YES...
NO WONDER YOU HAVE THAT EVIL-LOOKING FACE...
LOOK WHO'S TALKING.
BUT IF YOU HAVE ABANDONED BUDDHA...
KRAKL
KRAKL
...WHAT'S WITH THE TRAINING?
MY BELIEFS MAY HAVE BEEN ABANDONED... BUT NOT MY WILL TO SAVE THE WORLD.
AND IT CANNOT BE BY THE BUDDHA'S HAND.

ONLY THE HANDS OF *MEN* CAN SAVE THE WORLD OF MEN...
...BUT, TO DO SO, THEY MUST SURPASS THE GODS.
KRAKL
KRAKL
I TRY TO ATTAIN SUCH POWER.
SO YOU DIDN'T "FALL"...
...BY GIVING IN TO TEMPTATION.
DO YOU KNOW ABOUT THE MOVEMENT TO ABOLISH BUDDHISM OF 10 YEARS AGO?
NO POINT IN EXPLAINING, THEN.
WHATEVER. DOUBT I COULD DO ANYTHING ABOUT IT EVEN IF I *HAD*.
BY THE WAY...

...IF THAT THING YOU DID BACK THERE WASN'T HŌRIKI...
...DOES THAT MEAN A NON-BELIEVER LIKE ME CAN LEARN IT?
KRKL
KRKL
I WON'T TURN IT TO EVIL OR NOTHIN', SO...
WILL YOU TEACH ME?
WHY DO YOU DESIRE POWER?
WHAT, IS THIS ONE OF THOSE ZEN RIDDLES ...?
ANSWER.
WELL, TO PUT IT SIMPLY...

...I JUST WANT TO BE...

...MORE *POWERFUL* THAN I AM.

I GUESS.

"A MAN I FOUGHT BEFORE LEAVING TOKYO TOLD ME MY DEFENSE WAS WEAK. I'VE BEEN THINKING ABOUT IT FOR A WHILE...
"...BUT HIS STYLE ISN'T MINE."
HM
KK
BESIDES, I'D HATE TO GET BETTER BY LISTENING TO *HIM*.
HO-HO
MMG
...A VERY PERSONAL REASON.
WELL... COMPARED TO YOUR SAVING THE *WORLD*. YEAH.

READ THIS WAY

BUT TO ME...

...IT'S A REASON I'D GIVE MY *LIFE* FOR.

ANSWER ONE MORE.
WHAT DO YOU THINK OF THE MEIJI GOVERNMENT?

WHAT DOES THAT HAVE TO DO WITH—?
JUST ANSWER.
HONESTLY? I HATE IT.
IT *KILLED* MY CAPTAIN...
...AND *FRAMED* HIM AS AN IMPOSTER.
I WILL...
...*NEVER* FORGIVE THAT.

BUT WHAT DOES *THAT* HAVE TO DO WITH *THIS*?

LISTEN.
TO BREAK THIS ROCK, YOU APPLY FORCE TO IT WITH YOUR FIST.
BUT ALL OBJECTS, NOT JUST THIS ROCK, CARRY *RESISTANCE*—SO YOUR FORCE IS NOT FULLY TRANSFERRED TO THE OBJECT.

IN OTHER WORDS, SOME FORCE IS WASTED.

HOW DOES ONE AVOID THIS?
TEK
FIRST, YOU BRING YOUR FIST AGAINST THE ROCK LIKE THIS, AND DELIVER A FIRST IMPACT.

THEN, THE INSTANT THAT IMPACT MEETS THE ROCK'S RESISTANCE...
...YOU DELIVER A SECOND IMPACT BY FOLDING YOUR FIST. THAT IMPACT IS TRANSFERRED COMPLETELY WITHOUT HAVING TO HIT THE RESISTANCE...
TOK
...DESTROYING THE ROCK.

THAT IS THE SECRET I'VE DEVELOPED OVER 10 YEARS OF TRAINING...

"THE MASTERY OF TWO LAYERS."

WITH IT, ONE CAN PERFORM SUCH FEATS AS THE "DISTANT HIT" I WAS JUST ATTEMPTING.

THAT'S, UH...

...OVER-SIMPLIFIED...

RIGHT ??

TRY IT.

HH

GRAB

HSS...

...

HAH!

K-KOOOM

HUH?

IT DIDN'T SHATTER...

BECAUSE THAT WAS JUST TWO BLOWS.

KROMBLE KROMBLE

THE IMPACTS MUST BE QUICK. IT IS WITHIN A SETSUNA*...

SS

*1/75TH OF A SECOND

FROM THE TIME I UNDERSTOOD THIS SECRET, TO THE TIME I DESTROYED A ROCK...ONE MONTH.

YOU HAVE THE SAME.

MASTER IT WITHIN A MONTH... OR DIE HERE.

!

READ THIS WAY
THE "MASTERY OF TWO LAYERS" IS AN ABILITY DEVELOPED TO SAVE THE WORLD.
IT IS NOT SOMETHING I WANT TO SPREAD BY TEACHING TO JUST ANYONE.
YOU SAID YOU'D GIVE YOUR LIFE.
WOULD YOU?
YOU'RE A FALLEN PRIEST, ALL RIGHT.
"YOU WILL DIE" DOESN'T SOUND VERY PRIESTLY.
...FINE. I'LL GIVE MY LIFE.
GRIN
BUT I DON'T HAVE ANY TIME TO WASTE ON TRAINING!
I DON'T NEED A MONTH!
I'LL MASTER THIS "TWO LAYERS" STUFF WITHIN A WEEK!!

Rurouni
Kenshin

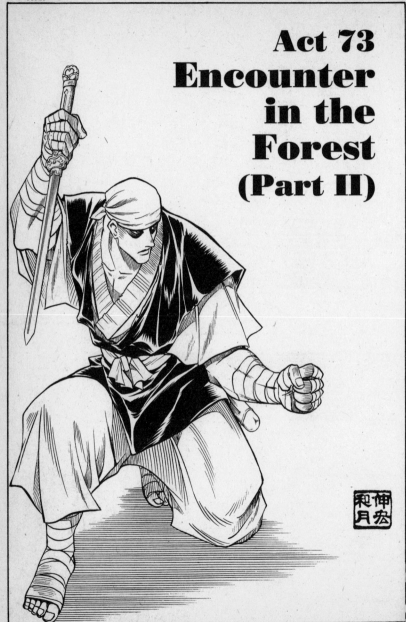

Act 73 Encounter in the Forest (Part II)

ORAH!
KROMB
KROMB
SINCE SANOSUKE BEGAN TRAINING IN THE "MASTERY OF TWO LAYERS"...
DAMN. STILL NOT WORKING RIGHT.
HF
HF
HF
...ALREADY THREE DAYS HAVE PASSED.
I DELIVERED THOSE TWO BLOWS SO FAST.
IT SHOULD BE EASY...BUT I CAN'T DO IT.
FOMP

EASIER SAID..
...THAN DONE.
ONE WEEK IS IMPOSSIBLE. YOU MUST RECONSIDER.
YOU MUST HAVE A FEELING FOR HOW DIFFICULT IT IS TO MAKE THE MASTERY A REALITY.
THERE ARE FOUR MORE DAYS TO THIS WEEK.
IN FOUR DAYS, "...EVEN THE PISS IN THE RIVER CAN FLOW TO THE SEA."
YOUR POINT BEING?
FORGET IT.
HEH!
...STUB-BORN MAN.

POSSIBLE OR *IM*-POSSIBLE...
...YOU CAN'T JUDGE UNTIL FOUR DAYS FROM NOW.
HEH
"PRAYERS IN A HORSE'S EAR."
SHH
WHO YOU CALLING A HORSE?
VERY WELL. THE TIME LIMIT IS ONE WEEK.
YOU'VE FOUR DAYS LEFT.
GG
IF YOU CANNOT PERFORM THE TWO-LAYERS STRIKE BY THEN...
...THEN I WILL SEE YOU *DEAD*, AS PROMISED.

YOU...
...ARE ON!
DAY FOUR
BRAK
IF IT'S SOMETHING I CAN GET *WITHOUT* BETTING MY LIFE, WHO NEEDS IT?!
THOOM
WHAT I WANT...
WHAT I'M SEEKING—

DAY FIVE
...YOU WON'T ATTAIN IT.
THE "MASTERY OF TWO LAYERS" IS THE *PINNACLE* OF 10 YEARS OF TRAINING.
"IT IS NOT SO CHEAP AS TO BE LEARNED ...
"...BY DESIRE ALONE".
DAY SIX
WOBBLE
SLAP
HUH
NOT... YET...
HUH

READ THIS WAY

THERE'S STILL TIME... TILL DAWN.
HF
HF
HF
NNN
...FEH.
I'VE CRUSHED EVERY DECENT ROCK IN THE AREA.

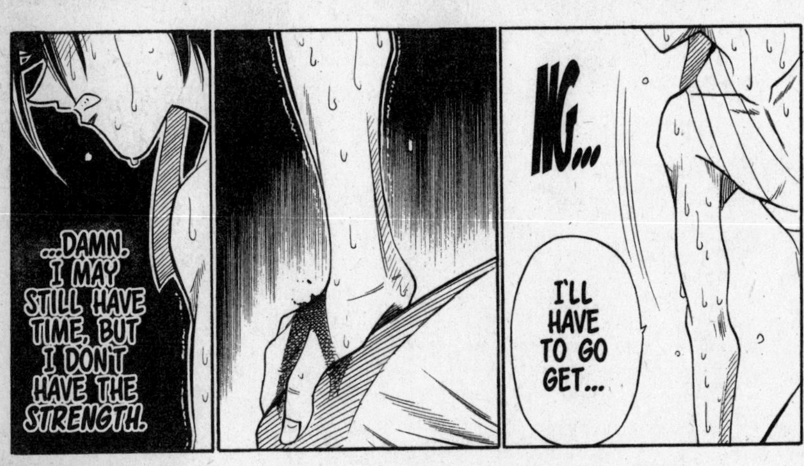

NG...
I'LL HAVE TO GO GET...
...DAMN. I MAY STILL HAVE TIME, BUT I DON'T HAVE THE STRENGTH.

WILL IT ALL END...
DAMN IT.
...IN THE MIDDLE OF NOWHERE LIKE THIS?

SANOSUKE
...

CAPTAIN...
...SAGARA
...?

AM I... DREAMING ...
...OR HALLUCI-NATING ...?
RUB
RUB

SWOO SWOO
SWOO

YAAAH!
NO FEET!
SKID SKID SKID

Long time no see. Watsuki here. By the time this volume hits store shelves [in Japan], the TV anime should be just starting. Let me say this right now, though—I have no control over the anime. There's no point in sending me letters about voice-actors, or what you hope to see animated—please direct those to the production company, and to the (Shueisha's) anime department. I'll take full responsibility for opinions, desires, and objections to the manga, but I can't take responsibility for how well or how badly the TV show turns out. I can believe only in the professionalism of the anime staff, and let them do their stuff. I'm hoping for the best possible outcome, of course—if it does badly, it'll affect Watsuki's career as a manga artist! Therefore, please watch at least 10 episodes or so, huh? See you.

IT'S ALL RIGHT, SANOSUKE.
YOU'VE DONE ENOUGH.
YOU'VE PUSHED YOURSELF TO YOUR LIMITS.
IF YOU ADMIT YOUR DEFEAT, HE PROBABLY WON'T TAKE YOUR LIFE.
IF YOU DO KEEP PUSHING YOURSELF ...
...THAT ITSELF MAY END YOUR LIFE.
JUST FORGET IT ALL... AND REST.
THAT'S AN ORDER.
...I'M SORRY, CAPTAIN.
I CANNOT OBEY...
...THAT ORDER.

BACK THEN...WHEN YOUR HEAD WAS *PUT UP* AS AN *EXAMPLE*...I *HATED* THE REVOLUTIONARY GOVERNMENT, FROM THE BOTTOM OF MY HEART...

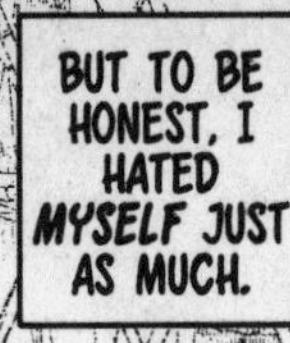

BUT TO BE HONEST, I HATED *MYSELF* JUST AS MUCH.

I WAS SO *ANGRY* WITH MYSELF FOR BEING UNABLE TO DO ANYTHING WHEN THE MAN I RESPECTED MORE THAN ANY OTHER WAS KILLED.

TEN YEARS LATER...AS I GREW MORE AND MORE BITTER... A *GOOD MAN* CAME, AND WOKE ME UP.

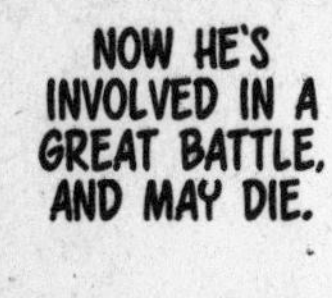

NOW HE'S INVOLVED IN A GREAT BATTLE, AND MAY DIE.

I DON'T WANT TO RELIVE...

...THE *RAGE* I KNEW 10 YEARS AGO.

"AND I WON'T LET ANYONE ELSE...

ORO!

"...KNOW THAT FEELING, EITHER."

THAT'S WHY I...

...HAVE GOT TO BECOME MORE POWERFUL... AND NOW.

THE POWER TO STRIKE AT ALL THE WORLD'S UNJUST VIOLENCE...

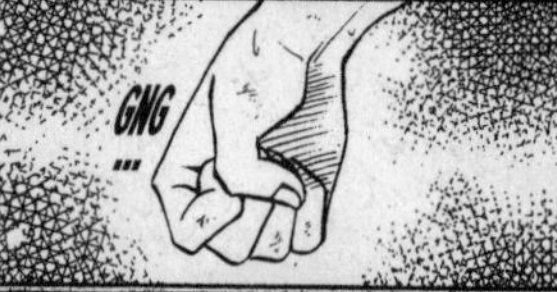

...WITH THIS VERY FIST...!

AS DREAM... HALLUCINATION...

...OR GHOST...

I'M HAPPY... TO SEE YOU AGAIN, HOWEVER SO.

READ THIS WAY

HE DIED FROM EXHAUSTION...
A SHAME TO LOSE HIM.
I MUST AT LEAST SAY A PRAYER...

DON'T KILL ME YET...
BLINK
I'M JUST... RESTING MY EYES, IS ALL.

...YOU NO-GOOD PRIEST.

YAWWN

UP

BUT... FROM THAT ROCK IN YOUR RIGHT HAND... I CAN SEE YOU WERE UNABLE TO MASTER THE TWO LAYERS.

FLIP

OH, I MASTERED IT, ALL RIGHT.
BUT ONCE I GOT THE HANG OF IT, SO WHAT?
...YOU HAVE *SOME* POTENTIAL.
...PRIEST. I ALMOST *DIED,* THERE.

DON'T YOU DEMEAN THAT...

...WITH A WORD LIKE "POTENTIAL."

HEHH

...YOU'RE RIGHT.

LET ME REPHRASE, THEN.

SWIP

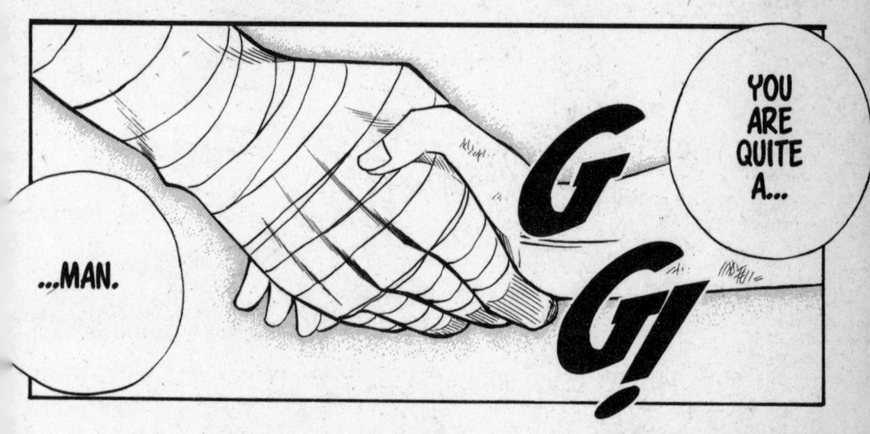

READ THIS WAY
THAT'S EASY.
THIS IS SHIMOSUWA, SO IF YOU GO THROUGH THE FOREST, THAT WAY, YOU'LL COME UPON THE INNS ON NAKASEN ROAD.
HEY...
DID YOU JUST SAY SHIMOSUWA?
YES.
WHAT OF IT?
WHAT THE—?
SHIMOSUWA!
HAAAA-HAHAHA!
NO WONDER IT LOOKED FAMILIAR!
IT'S STRANGE SAYING THIS TO A FALLEN PRIEST, BUT...
THIS WAS THE LAST STOP OF THE SEKIHŌ ARMY.
SUDDENLY, I FEEL A LITTLE LIKE BELIEVING IN HEAVENLY GUIDANCE.
?
IT'S ALL RIGHT. JUST FORGET IT.

THANKS FOR THE HOSPITALITY.

I'M SAGARA SANOSUKE, BY THE WAY.

LET'S MEET AGAIN IF WE'RE MEANT TO.

AND I AM YŪKYŪZAN ANJI.

FAREWELL.

OVERNIGHT HE'S BECOME A BIGGER MAN.

TM

TM

JUST THE OTHER DAY, HE WAS A MERE HATCHLING...

...AND YET, TODAY, HE'S LIKE A YOUNG BIRD LEAVING THE NEST.

OH, THERE YOU ARE.
I'VE BEEN LOOKING FOR YOU, ANJI-SAN.
SŌJIRŌ-DONO.

THE BATTLE IS BEGINNING.
THE ENTIRE "JUPPON-GATANA"...
...HAS BEEN SUMMONED TO KYOTO.

AND SO THE STAGE MOVES...

...TO THE TURBULENCE OF KYOTO.

The Secret Life of Characters (28)
—Yūkyūzan Anji—

This character had been almost entirely developed before the publication of "*RuroKen*"—to prove it, he appears in "*Rurouni*" as an extra (come to think of it, I think Sōjirō appears as an extra himself). When it came time to decide Anji's backstory, though, and to determine whether he was friend or foe, I couldn't quite pull it together and he stayed in storage... until now. As the story progressed, I felt the need for Sanosuke to become more powerful, so Anji appeared as a counterpart to Sanosuke's fighting style. That way, I was able to kill two birds (Sanosuke's power-up, and his need for a strong foe) with one stone... and it'll add depth to their battle, in the future. Anji carries a cross representing the Buddhism abolition movement, so the tension between them is going to be quite thick. (I want it to happen *now!*)

In terms of personality, there's no model, but I picture him somewhat like Shimada Kai—a Shinsengumi lieutenant—due to his manly air. Anji is also my second attempt at "macho intelligence," at which I failed quite utterly with Raijūta.

Unusual for Watsuki, his visual model came not from manga or a video game, but from the lead vocalist of a punk band called "Angie"—since disbanded. (I don't need to explain that "Anji" comes from "Angie," right?) With bandanas on shaved heads and black makeup beneath their eyes, somehow they still gave an impression of intelligence, and looked cool. When designing Anji, I wanted to make him a "power-fighter," but settled for macho, instead. I like their song "Silver Wristwatch" (it's a best-of-the-best), so give it a listen if you have the chance. Watsuki is greatly influenced by manga and video games, but Angie and Kin'niku Shojo-tai, another band, have influenced him a lot, too.

Act 74
Arrival
in Kyoto

WE'RE FINALLY HERE—!
I FEEL SO MUCH MORE AT *HOME* HERE.
TP
KYOTO ...

KYOTO
A CITY IN THE PLAINS OF THE KINKI REGION, A CENTER OF ARTS AND CRAFTS, AND OF BUDDHISM, AS WELL. IT HAS BEEN OVER A THOUSAND YEARS SINCE THE CAPITAL WAS MOVED ELSEWHERE (IN 794), THUS ITS OTHER NAME, SEN'NENOKI ("MILLENNIUM KING'S CASTLE").

TEN YEARS OF WANDERING SINCE THE REVOLUTION...

...AND NEVER DID THIS ONE THINK TO SET FOOT HERE AGAIN.

HIMURA, THIS WAY!

IN EVERY SEASON, ITS BEAUTY IS UNPARALLELED IN JAPAN, BUT...

...BEHIND ITS BEAUTY LURK MEMORIES OF EVIL, RESTLESS SPIRITS, ECHOING ITS CENTURIES OF FAMINE, PLAGUE, AND WAR.

DURING THE BAKUMATSU, KYOTO KNEW NO DAYS WITHOUT BLOODSHED AND ROLLING HEADS. IT WAS A PORTRAIT OF HELL.
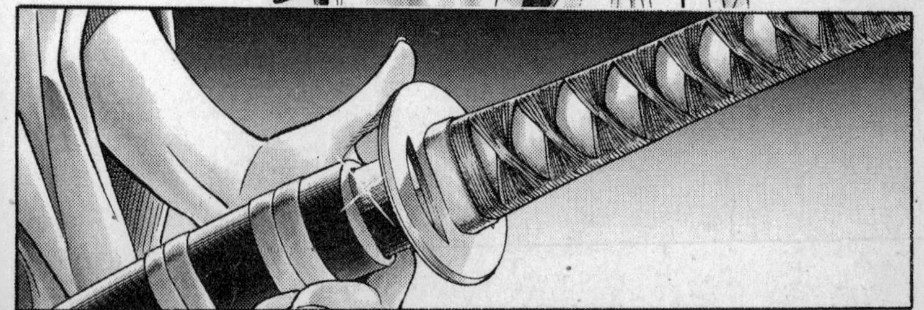

RA!!

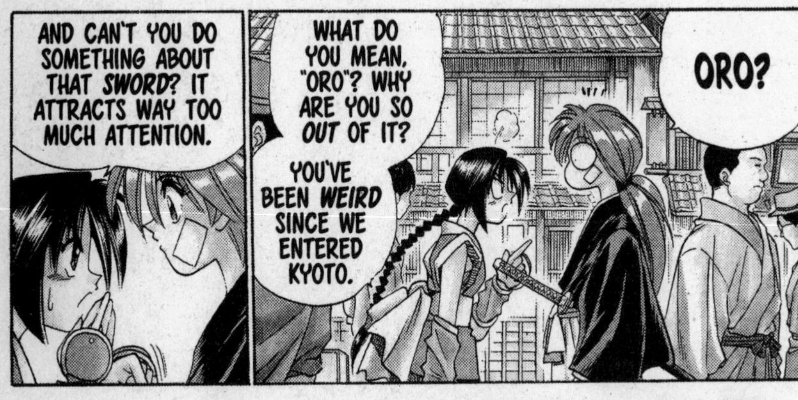
ORO?
WHAT DO YOU MEAN, "ORO"? WHY ARE YOU SO *OUT* OF IT?
YOU'VE BEEN *WEIRD* SINCE WE ENTERED KYOTO.
AND CAN'T YOU DO SOMETHING ABOUT THAT *SWORD*? IT ATTRACTS WAY TOO MUCH ATTENTION.
AND IF MISAO-DONO WERE PERHAPS TO CHANGE HER *OUTFIT*...
RG!
WHAT DID YOU...?!

"BIRD-KICK OF RAGE"!
BWAH-KAH
ORO!
CONCLUSION: IT'S THE TWO TOGETHER THAT'S THE PROBLEM.

REALLY, MISAO-DONO, YOU SHOULD HEAD HOME.
YOUR PEOPLE MUST BE GETTING WORRIED, AND...
...WHERE IS YOUR HOME?

RIGHT OVER THERE. WE'RE HERE ALREADY.
SEE?
ORO.

AN INN...

YUP. AOI-YA. WE'RE *FAMOUS* IN KYOTO.

...OH.

葵屋

葵屋

葵屋

GRAMPS! HEY—!

MISAO!!
WHOOO-
PUH-POP!

I'M HOME!
AND SO YOU ARE!!

YOU TOOK SO LONG, WE WERE TERRIFIED!
SORRY, SORRY! I WAS... DELAYED.
KRAK
OW OW OWOWOW OWOWOW OW OW!
KRAK KRAK KRAK
THIS IS FOR SCARING ME!
SKWEEZ
SKWEEZ
OOH. MAD. VERY.

...SO. YOU WALKED OUR MISAO HOME?
YES, WELL ...
MUST'VE BEEN HARD TO BE WITH HER.
IT WASN'T HARD. IT... IT WAS AWFUL!
DM DM
...
MISAO-CHAN!
LOOK WHO'S FINALLY HOME!

GASP

THEN IF YOU'LL EXCUSE...

HOLD ON, YOU! I HAVEN'T THANKED YOU YET.

SHIRO AND KURO WILL MAKE YOU THEIR BEST DINNER TONIGHT.
SHE'S ASKING YOU TO STAY.
YOU'LL LOVE IT!
PLEASE, MAKE YOURSELF AT HOME...
...HIMURA BATTŌSAI-DONO.

EVEN IF YOU HIDE YOUR SCARS...
...THOSE WHO CAN TELL, CAN TELL.
OLD MAN...
WE'LL TALK DETAILS INSIDE.
PLEASE COME IN.
MEAN-WHILE...
WOW, A CHOW-CHOW!
HF
HF
HOW NOW, CHOW-CHOW?
BOW, CHOW-CHOW, BOW!
BLAH BLAH
YOW—

IT'S...
...SOME KINDA FOREIGN TALK!

...KAORU AND YAHIKO HAVE ARRIVED IN KYOTO BY BOAT.
STILL, THIS IS THE MILLENNIUM ROYAL CASTLE...
IF I HADN'T HEARD IT WITH MY OWN EARS...
WILL YOU QUIT FOOLING AND HELP ME?!
WE HAVE TO FIND TAE-SAN'S FAMILY HOME.
LODGING'S TOO EXPENSIVE. I'LL TELL MY FAMILY YOU'LL BE STAYING WITH THEM.
BUT KYOTO ALL LOOKS THE SAME...
...IT'S SO HARD TO TELL...
...HOW CAN I EVER FIN SOMEONE IN THIS PLACE?
IDIOT!!
BCHONG
DON'T YOU CONK OUT AND LOSE THE ENERGY YOU JUST GOT BACK!
I'LL GO LOOK FOR TAE'S FAMILY—YOU WATCH THE PEOPLE!
IF WE'RE LUCKY, KENSHIN JUST MIGHT WALK BY!
CHING

WHEN I HEARD THE RING OF THAT *SWORD*, I THOUGHT...

I GUESS IT'S TOO GOOD TO BE TRUE.

WHY...

...IS *THAT MAN* IN KYOTO?

SO...
...FOR BRINGING OUR MISAO BACK SAFELY...
...AND FOR WITNESSING THE END OF THE ONIWABANSHŪ ...
TMM
...I SHALL EXTEND TO YOU MY FRIENDSHIP...
ORO?

I LIKE THE KYOTO OF TODAY.

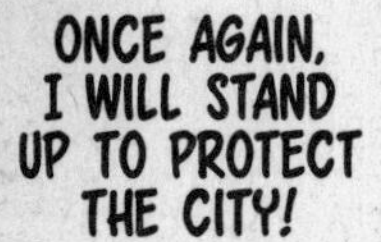

W... WAIT A SECOND...
DON'T YOU WORRY ABOUT AOI-YA.
HO HO HO
SHIRO, KURO, OKON, OMASU—ALL EX-ONIWABANSHŪ.
KURO
SHIRO
THEY CAN EASILY DEFEND MISAO AND THEMSELVES.
OMASU
OKON
STILL...
WIP
I WON'T HEAR ANOTHER WORD!
TOOM

READ THIS WAY
HEH
I'M THE ONE WHO RAISED MISAO, AFTER ALL.
STUBBORN TO THE BONE
ORO...
WEIRD... YET STRANGELY PERSUASIVE ...
YOU GOT IT.
HO HO HO
THEN... YOUR OFFER IS ACCEPTED...
ANY-THING YOU'D LIKE.
...WITH ONE CONDITION.
MIGHT YOUR INFORMATION NETWORK SEARCH FOR A COUPLE OF PEOPLE?
SEARCH?
YES.

ARAI SHAKKŪ AND HIKO SEIJŪRŌ.
FIND THEM...AS SOON AS YOU CAN.

Rurouni
Kenshin

Act 75
Searching for the Sakabatō

伸宏
和月

SECOND DAY IN KYOTO...
葵屋
WAKE UP, HIMURA!
IT'S MORNING, AND...
KLA TATT
HM?
—OH. YOU WERE ALREADY AWAKE?
I WANTED TO SEE YOUR SLEEPY FACE.
ORO?
MISAO-DONO—THAT OUTFIT!
IN KYOTO, THESE ARE MY STREET CLOTHES.
I CAN'T BE WALKING AROUND IN MY NINJA OUTFIT.
LA-LA-LAH!

IF YOU'RE READY, HIMURA-KUN, LET'S GO.
ORO.
KYOTO'S CHANGED A LOT IN 10 YEARS.
I'LL SPEND TODAY SHOWING YOU AROUND.
HEH

WE'LL GRAB LUNCH AT A LOCAL HOT-POT HOUSE, "SHIROBEKO."

YAY! BEEN WANTING TO EAT THERE!

OKINA-DONO, A MOMENT, PLEASE.

BUT TO JUST STROLL ABOUT KYOTO IN MID-DAY...
SHISHIO'S MEN MIGHT COME BY AT ANY TIME, OR—

SHISHIO IS YOUR OPPONENT. YOU CAN RUN, YOU CAN HIDE; EVENTUALLY, HE'LL STILL FIND YOU.
BUT—!

READ THIS WAY

HIMURA-KUN, YOU FIGHT SHISHIO FOR THE SAKE OF THE PEOPLE OF THIS COUNTRY.

WALK WITH PRIDE!

THAT'S HOW *RIGHTEOUS* MEN LIVE.

VIP

...
HO HO
HO HO
HO HO

I HAVE SOMETHING TO TELL YOU.
PSST!

"A LONG TIME AGO, GRAMPS WAS SO STRONG HE WAS EXPECTED TO BE THE NEXT OKASHIRA OF THE ONIWABANSHŪ.
"BUT GRAMPS SAID 'IT'S TIME FOR THE YOUNGER GENERATION TO TAKE CHARGE,' AND RECOMMENDED *AOSHI-SAMA* AS HEAD. INSTEAD, HE VOLUNTEERED TO BE OKASHIRA OF KYOTO INTELLIGENCE."

THOUGH HE MAY BE JUST A NUTJOB

HO
HO

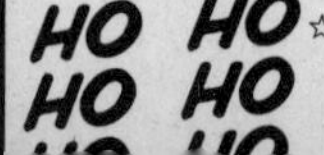
HO
HO

...OH, YEAH. ABOUT THE PEOPLE YOU'RE LOOKING FOR...

I MADE ARRANGEMENTS DURING THE NIGHT.

PEOPLE? WHO? WHA—?

IT HAS NOTHING TO DO WITH YOU.

WHAT KINDA CRACK IS THAT?!

OKINA.

HM ...?

HERE.

ZIP

RIP RIP

TWIK

MISAO, I'M SORRY. WE'LL GO TO SHIROBEKO ANOTHER TIME.

HIMURA-KUN.

WE HAVE FOUND ONE OF THE PEOPLE YOU'RE LOOKING FOR.

TO BE MORE PRECISE...
...WE'VE CONFIRMED HIS DEATH.
ARAI SHAKKŪ, THE SWORDSMITH WHO FORGED YOUR SAKABATŌ...
...DIED EIGHT YEARS AGO.

"SWORD-SMITH"... I-I-I GET IT.
YOU WERE GONNA HAVE HIM MAKE A REPLACEMENT FOR THE SAKABATŌ...!
BUT... IF HE'S DEAD...
...THE SAKABATŌ WILL NEVER BE...!

THIS IS IT.
TAE-SAN'S FAMILY HOME... "SHIROBEKO."
京風 牛鍋
白べこ
IT'S SISTER-SHOP TO AKABEKO IN TOKYO.
EXCUSE ME.
*LAST NIGHT WAS SPENT AT AN INN.
WELCOME.
!
TAE-SAN?!
WHY ARE YOU IN KYOTO?!

TAE?
OH-H-H, YOU MUST BE THE TWO COMING FROM TOKYO!
UM
UH
I'M TAE'S TWIN SISTER, SAE.
PLEASED TO MEET YOU.
TAE'S LETTER TOLD ME ALL ABOUT YOU.
YOU'VE BEEN THROUGH A LOT, HUH?
WELL, EVERYONE AT SHIROBEKO...
...WILL TREAT YOU JUST AS TAE WOULD HAVE!
THANKS!

READ THIS WAY

JUST HANG ON, KENSHIN!!

ALL THAT'S LEFT TO DO NOW IS FIND KENSHIN...

...BEFORE SHISHIO, OR AOSHI.

ARAI SHAKKŪ.

HE WAS A HIGHLY HONORED WEAPONS-MAKER DURING THE BAKUMATSU.

BUT, AS YEARS WENT BY, HE DEVOTED HIMSELF NOT TO "BLADES THAT CUT," BUT TO "BLADES THAT KILL," AND THEREAFTER WAS SHUNNED...

...BY THE REST OF THE SWORD-CRAFTING COMMUNITY.

A SMITH WHO SPECIALIZED IN *KILLING SWORDS* FORGED THE SAKABATŌ?
I DON'T GET IT.
A MAN'S LIFE CAN AT TIMES SEEM QUITE CONTRADICTORY...
...RIGHT, HIMURA-KUN?

TO CONTINUE...

ACCORDING TO OUR SOURCES, SHAKKŪ HAS ONE SON TO WHOM HE TAUGHT EVERYTHING HE KNEW.

HE WAS EXPECTED TO BECOME A SWORDSMITH HIMSELF...BUT, IN THE MEIJI ERA, HE COULDN'T MAKE A LIVING AT THAT...

...SO HE SELLS *TOOLS* LIKE SCYTHES AND KNIVES TO SUPPORT HIMSELF.

SHAKKŪ'S SON...
...IS ARAI SEIKŪ.
PERHAPS THIS MAN CAN CRAFT A NEW SAKABATŌ!

EXCUSE THE...
SHP

Bwah!
SEIKŪ?
Bwah?
WHAT THE...

READ THIS WAY

GRAB GRAB

OH-H-H, SHAKE HANDS. RIGHT, RIGHT.
SHAKE HANDS.
Buh.

NOW, IORI, DON'T BOTHER THEM.

WELCOME. WHAT MAY I HELP YOU WITH...?

IF A KITCHEN KNIFE MIGHT BE PRESENTED...

HIMURA-KUN?
AND GIVEN A BRIEF TEST OF EDGE...
SURE.

TUG
!
?
?
ZUP
PING
!!!

READ THIS WAY

A "REVERSING CUT." FIRST TIME I'VE SEEN IT.

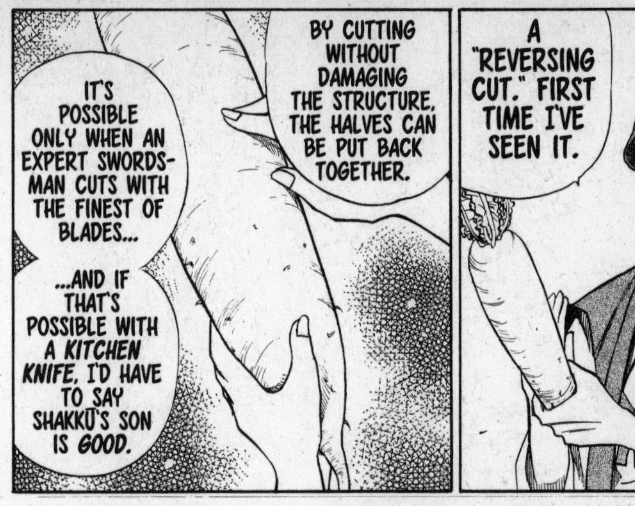
BY CUTTING WITHOUT DAMAGING THE STRUCTURE, THE HALVES CAN BE PUT BACK TOGETHER.
IT'S POSSIBLE ONLY WHEN AN EXPERT SWORDS-MAN CUTS WITH THE FINEST OF BLADES...
...AND IF THAT'S POSSIBLE WITH A *KITCHEN KNIFE*, I'D HAVE TO SAY SHAKKŪ'S SON IS *GOOD*.

WHOA! *TOO* GOOD!
THE NEW SAKABATŌ JUST *HAS* TO BE MADE BY ARAI SEIKŪ!

MADAM, MIGHT SEIKŪ-DONO BE AVAILABLE?
YES...
IF SEIKŪ-DONO MIGHT CRAFT A SWORD...
...IT WOULD BE FINE, INDEED.

YES... BUT...

HM?

TP

SEIKŪ.

Paah!

HELLO...

I AM ARAI SEIKŪ.

YOU'RE SEIKŪ?
YOU DON'T SEEM LIKE HIM.
MM...
...I HEAR THAT A LOT.
I HEARD YOUR STORY FROM OUTSIDE.
IT SEEMS THAT YOU'D LIKE ME TO FORGE A SWORD, BUT...

...I APOLOGIZE. I HAVE QUIT MAKING SWORDS.
YOU'LL HAVE TO GO ELSEWHERE.

WHAT ?!
AUGH!
SORRY... SORRY!
HELP!

MAY WE HEAR YOUR REASON?
MMG

IF YOU'VE COME TO GET A SWORD OUT OF ME... ...YOU MUST KNOW THAT MY FATHER, SHAKKU, CREATED WEAPONS OF DEATH.

'FATHER USED TO SAY, ALL THE TIME...
"...'THE SWORDS I MAKE WILL CREATE A NEW AGE.'
"BUT I DIDN'T LIKE MY FATHER'S PHILOSOPHY."

"THOSE SWORDS INTENDED TO *CREATE* THAT NEW AGE TOOK MANY PEOPLE'S LIVES.
"WHAT KIND OF 'NEW AGE' DOES ONE FORGE FROM HUMAN BLOOD...?
"THAT, I COULD NEVER UNDER-STAND."
IT WAS A TERRIBLE TIME THEN, SO PERHAPS IT COULDN'T BE HELPED...
...BUT THIS IS MEIJI.
AN AGE OF PEACE, AT LAST.

THE SAMURAI HAVE GIVEN UP THEIR SWORDS.
SO, SIMILARLY, I HAVE GIVEN UP SWORD-MAKING...
...AND HAVE DECIDED TO LIVE *PEACEFULLY*, CRAFTING TOOLS FOR A LIVING.

I SEE. UNLIKE YOUR FATHER, *YOUR* PHILOSOPHY IS *PEACE*.
HMPH.
I DON'T KNOW ABOUT PHILOSOPHY...

...BUT I DO LIKE PEACE.
DOESN'T EVERYONE?

IDIOT!! YOU ARE SO NAÏVE!!
"DOESN'T EVERYONE"?! THIS CITY'S *FULL* OF PEOPLE WHO—
UNDERSTOOD, SEIKŪ-DONO.
MMPF
SORRY TO HAVE ASKED.
WE'LL BE LEAVING NOW.
"LEAVING"?! HIMURA-A-A!!
HEY!!
FROM HIS HEART, WHAT SEIKŪ-DONO WISHES FOR IS *PEACE.*
EVEN IF IT IS A SAKABATŌ, AND NOT FOR KILLING, IT'S STILL A WEAPON.
IT WOULD BE *WRONG* TO ASK HIM TO CRAFT SUCH A THING.
WE'LL HAVE TO START ALL OVER...
...ON THE SEARCH FOR A SAKABATŌ.

THAT SWORDS-MAN...
HM?
Fuah.
...CAME HERE SPECIFICALLY LOOKING FOR YOU. WHAT IF HE HAS SOME DIRE NEED?

EVEN IF YOU WOULDN'T FORGE A SWORD...
..COULDN'T YOU AT LEAST AVE GIVEN HIM YOUR FATHER'S LAST WORK?

...NO.
THIS IS RIGHT.

IN PEACEFUL MEIJI...
Fuah.
Fuah.
...THERE IS NO NEED FOR SWORDS ANYMORE.

BATTŌSAI HAS BEEN SEEN. REPORT TO SHISHIO-SAMA IM-MEDIATELY.
AT LAST...

GLOSSARY of the RESTORATION

A brief guide to select Japanese terms used in **Rurouni Kenshin**. *Note that, both here and within the story itself, all names are Japanese style—i.e., last or "family" name first, with personal or "given" name following. This is both because* **Kenshin** *is a "period" story, as well as to decrease confusion—if we were to take the example of Kenshin's* sakabatô *and "reverse" the format of the historically established assassin-name "Hitokiri Battôsai," for example, it would make little sense to then call him "Battôsai Himura."*

Hiten Mitsurugi-ryû
Kenshin's sword technique, used more for defense than offense. An "ancient style that pits one against many," it requires exceptional speed and agility to master.

hitokiri
An assassin. Famous swordsmen of the period were sometimes thus known to adopt "professional" names—***Kawakami Gensai***, for example, was also known as "Hitokiri Gensai."

Ishin Shishi
Loyalist or pro-Imperialist ***patriots*** who fought to restore the Emperor to his ancient seat of power

Kamiya Kasshin-ryû
Sword-arts or ***kenjutsu*** school established by Kaoru's father, who rejected the ethics of ***Satsujin-ken*** for ***Katsujin-ken***

Kansatsu Tobikunai
"Piercing/Killing Flying Daggers." Misao's special technique

katana
Traditional Japanese longsword (curved, single-edge, worn cutting-edge up) of the samurai. Used primarily for slashing; can be wielded either one- or two-handed

Katsujin-ken
"Swords that give life"; the sword-arts style developed over ten years by Kaoru's father and founding principle of ***Kamiya Kasshin-ryû***

Kawakami Gensai
Real-life, historical inspiration for the character of ***Himura Kenshin***

Bakumatsu
Final, chaotic days of the Tokugawa regime

"Bird-kick of rage!"
Fans of the video game "Street Fighter" will remember that one of the special moves of the character Chun-Li was the Spinning Bird-Kick.

-chan
Honorific. Can be used either as a diminutive (e.g., with a small child—"Little Hanako or Kentarô"), or with those who are grown, to indicate affection ("My dear...")

dirt dumplings
That which you eat when you've nothing *else* to eat... a kind of "mud pies," maybe?

dojo
Martial arts training hall

-dono
Honorific. Even more respectful than ***–san***; the effect in modern-day Japanese conversation would be along the lines of "Milord So-and-So." As used by Kenshin, it indicates both respect and humility

Edo
Capital city of the ***Tokugawa Bakufu***; renamed ***Tokyo*** ("Eastern Capital") after the Meiji Restoration

Himura Battôsai
Swordsman of legendary skills and former assassin (***hitokiri***) of the ***Ishin Shishi***

Himura Kenshin
Kenshin's "real" name, revealed to Kaoru only at her urging

sakabatô
Reversed-edge sword (the dull edge on the side the sharp should be, and vice-versa); carried by Kenshin as a symbol of his resolution never to kill again

-san
Honorific. Carries the meaning of "Mr.," "Ms.," "Miss," etc., but used more extensively in Japanese than its English equivalent (note that even an enemy may be addressed as "***-san***")

Satsujin-ken
"Swords that give death"; a style of swordsmanship rejected by Kaoru's father

Shinsengumi
"True to the old ways and risking their lives to preserve the old shôgunate system," the popular view of the Shinsengumi ("newly elected group") was that of swordsmen as charismatic as they were skilled. Of note: Thanks to the popularity of the NHK drama of the same name, several historical sites in Japan are reportedly enjoying record attendance levels of late.

shôgun
Feudal military ruler of Japan

shôgunate
See ***Tokugawa Bakufu***

Tokugawa Bakufu
Military feudal government which dominated Japan from 1603 to 1867

Tokyo
The renaming of "***Edo***" to "***Tokyo***" is a marker of the start of the ***Meiji Restoration***

Wolves of Mibu
Nickname for the ***Shinsengumi***, so called because of the town (Mibu) where they were first stationed

"weasel girl" (itachi musume)
The author makes a joke, comparing in the previous panel Misao to a weasel, Kaoru to a *tanuki* or "raccoon-dog," and Megumi to a *kitsune* ("fox"... thus the "vixen" Kaoru always calls her). As much having to do with their personalities as any physical resemblance, Watsuki's humor here echoes the recurring joke about Sano ("*tori-atama*" or "chicken/bird-head").

-kun
Honorific. Used in the modern day among male students, or those who grew up together, but another usage—the one you're more likely to find in *Rurouni Kenshin*—is the "superior-to-inferior" form, intended as a way to emphasize a difference in status or rank, as well as to indicate familiarity or affection.

kunoichi
Female ninja. In that they are not referred to as simply "*onmitsu*"(ninja), their special name suggests their relative scarcity.

loyalists
Those who supported the return of the Emperor to power; ***Ishin Shishi***

Meiji Restoration
1853-1868; culminated in the collapse of the ***Tokugawa Bakufu*** and the restoration of imperial rule. So called after Emperor Meiji, whose chosen name was written with the characters for "culture and enlightenment"

onsen
Written in Japanese with the characters for "warmth" and "springs," ***onsen*** are an important part of Japanese tradition—both in the Meiji Era, and in present day. Ideally located outdoors amidst a scene of natural beauty, ***onsen*** are enjoyed both for their sociability (it's easier to "get real" with someone when neither of you is wearing clothes), as well as for their health benefits... the reason, in the story, for Shishio's visit to one.

patriots
Another term for ***Ishin Shishi***... and when used by Sano, not a flattering one

rurouni
Wanderer, vagabond

ryûshôsen
Sometimes translated as "Soaring Dragon Flash," the ***ryûshôsen*** of Kenshin's Hiten Mitsurugi school is one of his special moves, and is also known as "Dragon Flight"

IN THE NEXT VOLUME...

In search of a replacement *sakabatô*, Kenshin is turned away. Seikû, son of the legendary swordsmith, no longer continues his father's work, limiting his considerable skill to cooking knives and other implements only. As Shishio arrives at last in Kyoto, Chô, one of Shishio's "Ten Swords" or *Juppongatana*, learns of a final master blade and is determined to secure it at any cost. Now, armed only with his broken *sakabatô*, Kenshin and Chô square off in battle....

Available in January 2005

VIZ
LUFFY AND HIS CREW
CATCH BLACK CAT FEVER!
Only
$7.95
Each!
Volumes 1-5
on Sale Now!
ONE PIECE
SHONEN JUMP
GRAPHIC NOVELS
Now Airing
on the FoxBox!
On Sale At:
www.shonenjump.com
Also available at your local
bookstore, comic store and
Suncoast Motion Picture Company.
888-266-4226

A new reality show's in town, and Ichigo's about to make his prime-time debut!
BLEACH
ブリーチ
Only $7.95 Each!
VIZ
Vol. 1-4 Available Now!
BLEACH
ブリーチ
SHONEN JUMP GRAPHIC NOVEL
Tite Kubo
volume 4
SHONEN JUMP
GRAPHIC NOVELS
BLEACH © 2001 by TITE KUBO / SHUEISHA Inc.
COVER ART SUBJECT TO CHANGE.